THE ROAR OF
THE CROWD

THE ROAR OF THE CROWD

NEW ZEALAND RUGBY'S GREATEST PLAYERS, FAMOUS GAMES AND MEMORABLE MOMENTS

BOB HOWITT

PENGUIN BOOKS

ACKNOWLEDGEMENTS

The author wishes to thank Lindsay Knight who contributed a number of the features in the Games and Moments chapters and Denis Edwards and Margot Butcher who each weighed in with a story for the Moments section.

Thanks also to Bob Luxford of the New Zealand Rugby Museum in Palmerston North for his tireless and enthusiastic efforts in sourcing so many vital items and treasured photographs.

Professional photographers and agencies whose works have enhanced this publication are Andrew Cornaga (Photosport), John Selkirk (Dominion), Paddy Dillon (Pro Sport), Fotopress and News Media (Auckland).

S.R.F.U.

Official Programme.   Price 6d.

RANFURLY SHIELD CHALLENGE

MANAWATU

v.

SOUTHLAND

at 2.45 p.m.

SECOND GRADE MATCH

Bluff v. Invercargill

1 p.m.

—— • ——

RUGBY PARK,
INVERCARGILL

Sat., 12th August, 1939

NEWS PRINT.

CONTENTS

THE MOMENTS 109

INTRODUCTION

I WAS HOOKED ON RUGBY, I'm sure, before Bob Scott arrived in my 'village' of Petone in the mid-fifties. After all, from the age of five, I was running round like a demented gnat in a Petone rugby jersey. I used to listen, enthralled, to rugby commentaries beaming in, on our staticky radio, whenever the All Blacks played at home or away.

But it was Bob Scott's presence that secured my everlasting commitment to rugby. A wizened old Welshman assured me, when I was in Cardiff for the 1999 World Cup, that God had given Graham Henry to Wales. Well, back in 1955, if someone had offered a similar sentiment linking The Master to Petone, I would have understood absolutely.

From the old grandstand at the Petone Recreation Ground, I marvelled at the wizardry of Scott, at his deft ability to elude defenders, to nonchalantly gather high kicks and to always clear his line. In addition to which, he kept the scoreboard clicking over by landing goals from up to halfway. If that wasn't enough, he used to entertain at half-time in benefit matches by kicking goals barefooted from halfway (using the old-fashioned toe method). Imagine the impact that had on us young kids!

Petone boasted a rich rugby tradition and Bob Scott utterly electrified the place. The moment it was announced he was transferring to the capital from Auckland—at the not inconsiderable age, for a footballer, of 34—the place went mad. Season tickets were sold out virtually overnight and every time Petone staged a home game, the ground was packed out. The instant he ran out on to Petone Rec, the crowd roared. And they continued to roar every time he was involved in the action. I was among the roarers as Petone swept inexorably to championship success; indeed, in 1955, I was convinced that Robert William Henry Scott was the greatest rugby player the world had seen. There would surely never be another like him.

Well, a career in sports journalism would soon broaden the author's horizons, enabling him to identify other gifted rugby players with that rare capacity to make the crowd roar whenever they became involved in the action.

It soon became apparent that New Zealand rugby has been blessed with a generous number of these legendary characters, whose greatness, almost without exception, has been recognised well beyond the shores of their home land.

They were the spark for this book, the individuals whose achievements in the black jersey allowed New Zealand to stay at or near the top of the international rugby ladder throughout the 20th century—from heroes like

George Nepia, Bert Cooke and Maurice Brownlie of the 1920s through to modern day superstars such as Jonah Lomu, Michael Jones and Jeff Wilson.

Perhaps the greatest of them all was Colin 'Pinetree' Meads, recently named All Black of the Century. It was an award that seemed to sit comfortably with the nation. He is among the 22 who feature in this book, along with such icons of his era as Don Clarke, Brian Lochore, Waka Nathan, Kel Tremain and Wilson Whineray.

It's not always individuals who create the headlines in rugby (or sport generally); oft-times it's the match itself or events surrounding it. During the past century New Zealand rugby featured its share of unforgettable contests at representative and international level and more than a spattering of happenings that projected the game on to the front pages and often on to the billboards.

Fifteen of the most notable games have been selected, a third of these not surprisingly involving the Ranfurly Shield, a trophy which has been synonymous with drama, excitement and controversy since it was presented by the Earl of Ranfurly back in 1902. The fact that the trophy arrived from the UK featuring soccer goalposts and a round ball should have alerted New Zealand rugby fans to the fact that challenge matches for the shield would always be pretty special.

Rugby headlines haven't always been created by onfield deeds of players or the particular fortunes of teams. Many's the time they have evolved from moments of a sensational, unusual or downright bizarre nature.

Over the years there have been international matches staged in hurricanes and on flooded surfaces, a shield match fought out in 10 inches of snow, Springbok matches abandoned and others witnessed by no more than 30 spectators and, of course, there was the infamous Cavaliers tour of South Africa, undertaken by the pseudo All Blacks without the authority of their governing body.

This book has sought to capture many of the diverse happenings which have gone together to make rugby the enchanting sport it is, a sport with the capacity to suspend an entire nation when an All Black test match is being played. A sport that like no other in New Zealand gives rise to *The Roar of the Crowd*.

BOB HOWITT

THE PLAYERS

DO THEY PLAY rugby in heaven? Is there perhaps a set of goalposts in the hereafter where rugby players, eternally free of strained hamstrings, sniping critics, zealous administrators, inclement conditions and professionalism, could perform at the peak of their powers?

Then, and only then—when the finest footballers of the 20th century have all assembled—would it be possible to bring together the ultimate All Black fifteen.

Imagine a backline that featured the courageous George Nepia at fullback, the unstoppable Jonah Lomu on one wing and the side-stepping Beegee on the other, midfielders of the calibre of Bruce Robertson and Bert Cooke along with the supreme general Grant Fox at first-five outside Super Sid Going.

Up front, what riches—a pack built around Pinetree Meads, Sean Fitzpatrick, Wilson Whineray and Brian Lochore, with breakaways of the calibre of Maurice Brownlie and Michael Jones.

Ah, what a mouth-watering prospect. But because few if any rugby correspondents are likely to make it to the hallowed gates—and if they did, they would have to surrender their laptops, microphones, cameras and mobile phones—the outcome of such a game would remain unrecorded.

Which is probably as well. It leaves us mere mortals free to romance forever on the relative qualities of New Zealand's greatest rugby players. It doesn't matter whether Michael Jones of the eighties was a better flanker than Maurice Brownlie of the twenties, or whether George Nepia was a more heroic fullback than Bob Scott or the big-booting Don Clarke. They are all legends and their stories make fascinating reading.

For this chapter, 22 of the most celebrated All Blacks have been chosen, from Nepia, Brownlie and Cooke in the twenties through to the modern day heroes Lomu and Jeff Wilson.

Collectively, they are a reminder of how blessed New Zealand rugby has been through the decades in producing players of exceptional quality and skill, individuals who have helped ensure the All Blacks have always stayed close to being the best rugby team on earth.

COLIN MEADS

Voted All Black of the Century by the New Zealand public

Elsewhere in this book we write enthusiastically of the drop-kicking ability of Zinzan Brooke. Well, he's not the only famous All Black forward to land a dropped goal in a first-class fixture. Colin 'Pinetree' Meads managed it in his rep debut.

'I'm not sure which is the more remarkable fact,' says Meads. 'That I landed a dropped goal in my first game for King Country or that I didn't kick another one in my next 359 first-class outings!'

Meads was just 18 when he first pulled on the King Country jersey as a lock against Counties at Te Kuiti back in 1955. 'Things dropped into place pretty well,' he recalls. 'I was late for a ruck and received the ball in the equivalent of a first-five position. I honestly didn't know what to do, so from about 20 metres out I dropped a goal!'

He also scored a try that afternoon, making sufficient impact to impress Jack Finlay who alerted New Zealand selector Jack Sullivan to the presence of 'a fellow up north with a ton of potential'. That phone call would help launch the career of the individual who would become arguably the greatest All Black of all. Meads would represent his country for 15 seasons and establish an appearance record of 133 matches which, 28 years after his retirement, survives (even Sean Fitzpatrick, who seemed to go on forever, fell five appearances short of Meads's mark).

Only a few months after that eye-catching opener at Te Kuiti, Meads was touring Ceylon with the New Zealand Colts, giving coach J. J. Stewart an insight into his rich potential. Within two years, he was touring Australia as a 20-year-old, instantly claiming test selection. Although initially used as a flanker and a No. 8, he eventually settled into his best position of lock. From there, Meads became a permanent fixture in the All Blacks for 15 years, ringing down the curtain on an amazing career as captain against the 1971 British Lions.

When Meads was at the pinnacle of his powers in the sixties (and locking the scrum with his brother Stan) the All Blacks were nigh unbeatable. Indeed, until the Lions toppled Meads's men in 1971, the only significant setbacks in his vast international career were on the two tours (10 years apart) of South Africa.

He would also tour South Africa once more, controversially in 1986 as coach of the Cavaliers. This led to his sacking as an All Black selector by the NZRFU. Nor was that his greatest claim to notoriety. On the 1963–4 tour, he was ordered off during the match against Scotland at Murrayfield by Irish referee Kevin Kelleher for indiscriminate kicking.

If these were the low points, the balance of Meads's unparalleled career was awash with highlights, prompting fullback great Fergie McCormick to say of him that he regarded the All Black jersey as pure gold. 'He stood alone as the greatest player I have ever known.' Coach Fred Allen described him as 'stupendously consistent'. For many, the greatest sight in rugby was Meads in full flight, ball in hand. His greatness survived. In 1999, he was voted All Black of the Century.

Following his celebrated playing career, he coached at representative level and became a distinguished national administrator and All Black manager. His autobiography, published in 1974, sold 57,000 copies—testimony to his greatness.

Meads contests lineout possession at Wellington in 1968 with his great rival Frenchman Benoit Dauga.

STATISTICS

	Period	Games	Tries	Conv	DG	Points
Tests	57-71	55	7	-	-	21
NZ	57-71	133	28	1	-	86
Total	55-72	361	80	1	1	248

Above: *Colin Meads, at his rampaging best, scores a try against the 1966 British Lions at Athletic Park. Mike Gibson, Colin McFadyean and Jim Telfer (8) can only look on.*
Opposite: *In the mid-1960s the All Blacks were almost invincible—thanks to individuals like Meads (in possession), Ken Gray and Bruce McLeod.*

A programme from Pinetree's first season with King Country in 1955, when he was 19.

15

JOHN KIRWAN

Few players have enjoyed more spectacular rises to stardom than JK, the thoroughbred winger

John Kirwan, whose name still sits atop the All Black try-scorers' list, can reflect on an intriguing football career that spans four distinct phases.

For the greater part of his time as an Auckland and New Zealand representative—when he scored 50 test tries and more than 100 tries for Auckland—he was a true blue amateur, pocketing no more than the modest daily allowance given to All Blacks when they were on tour.

Many of his off-seasons were spent in Italy where clubs, with a blissful disregard for the game's laws of amateurism, were prepared to reward him with accommodation, a car and enough pocket money to live comfortably. It didn't make him rich but it allowed him to enjoy fully the Italian lifestyle.

The third phase of Kirwan's sporting career involved serious money when the Auckland Warriors offered him a contract to play league. Having been cast aside by the then All Black coach Laurie Mains, he decided to try his luck at the 13-a-side code, emerging as the club's leading try-scorer in 1996. He adopted a completely different mindset once he found himself playing for money. 'Suddenly I was a full-time sportsman,' he says. 'I was being paid for performing—I was no longer out there just to amuse myself and entertain.'

While Kirwan, or JK as everyone called him, was chancing his arm at league, rugby virtually overnight went fully professional. So after two years dabbling in league, Kirwan decided to cash in and accept an offer as player-coach of the NEC club in Japan, a position previously held by Joe Stanley. It represented an exciting new challenge for the fellow who started his working life as a butcher's

apprentice in his father's shop in Onehunga but whose footballing talents would make him a household name throughout the rugby world.

There have been few more spectacular rises to stardom than that enjoyed by Kirwan. In 1983 he was plucked from the Marist third-grade club team by John Hart and elevated to Auckland representative status, making his debut in the centennial fixture against a President's XV at Eden Park.

Fourteen months later, aged just 19, he would make his All Black debut against France at Lancaster Park. If the selectors were unsure whether to risk someone so young, Kirwan provided the answer when he scored a hat-trick of tries in the trial match in Hamilton, earning a standing ovation for his breathtaking achievements.

Although a seriously damaged shoulder would cut short his 1994 season, Kirwan would remain an automatic test selection for the All Blacks for nine seasons until Mains dropped him for the 1993 tour of England and Scotland. He became the darling of Eden Park, wowing fans with his try-scoring exploits through the halcyon Ranfurly Shield days of the late eighties. The *Rugby Annual* wrote of him in 1986 that 'Eden Park came alive every time he touched the ball'.

He remembers the 1987 World Cup triumph as 'the sort of dream from which you never want to wake up'. The All Blacks demolished every opponent, scoring 43 tries while conceding four, with Kirwan firmly establishing himself as the best winger in the world. His 100-metre try against Italy in the tournament opener is right up among the game's all-time great achievements.

Kirwan remains the leading All Black tryscorer—67 in all matches including 35 in tests—and this touchdown against Italy in the 1987 World Cup at Eden Park is arguably the greatest of them.

John Kirwan became the darling of Eden Park in the 1980s with his phenomenal achievements for Auckland and New Zealand.

Kirwan combined pace and strength. He was adept at pushing off opponents and off-loading to teammates as these scenes from the All Blacks against the Springboks and Auckland against King Country illustrate.

18

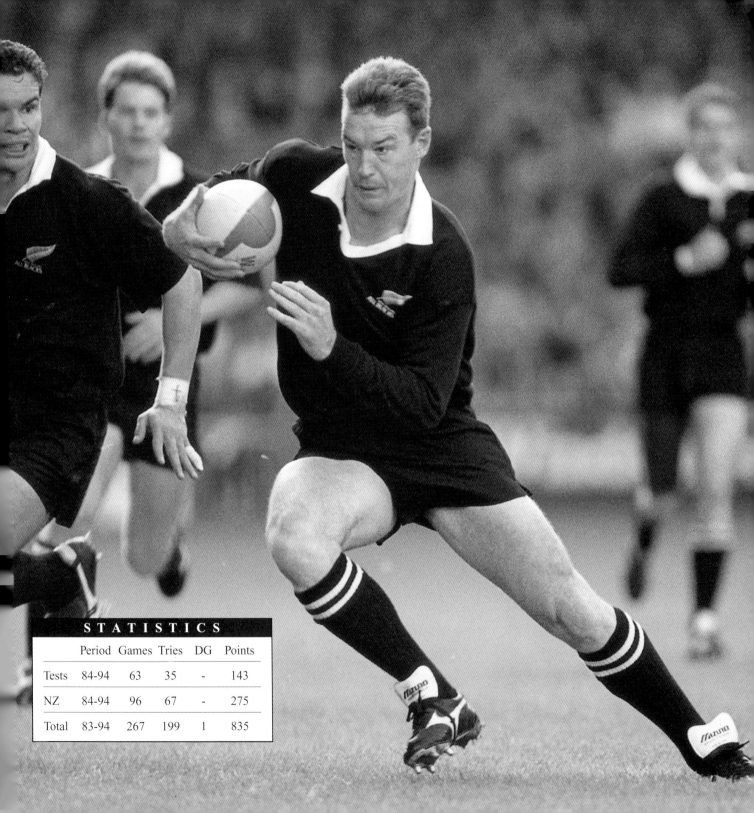

STATISTICS

	Period	Games	Tries	DG	Points
Tests	84-94	63	35	-	143
NZ	84-94	96	67	-	275
Total	83-94	267	199	1	835

DON CLARKE

The Boot broke the heart of countless opponents with his prodigious kicking

Big isn't always best. But there have been a couple of famous examples in New Zealand rugby where the adage about size does ring true.

Just ask anyone who's tried to tackle Jonah Lomu head on—England fullback Mike Catt, for example. A rampaging 118-kilogram winger represents an awesome challenge for an opponent of average physical proportions.

It was the same almost 40 years ago when Don 'The Boot' Clarke wore the No. 1 jersey which until 1965 was always allocated to the fullback. Big Don weighed in at around 111 kilograms and certainly imposed himself on a game.

In those days fullbacks knew their place, which was as the 'Last Line'. Fullbacks were known to be ticked off by their coaches and captains for daring to leave their station and run with the backs. It wasn't until Fergie McCormick entered the scene in 1967 with license to run—from coach Fred Allen who was promoting the 15-man game—that the fullback started to become an attacking weapon.

In Clarke's time, from the mid-fifties to the early sixties, the fullback was expected to field the high kicks, punt accurately to touch, tackle and, usually, kick the goals. Big Don fulfilled those duties spectacularly well, particularly the goal-kicking and punting. He could rake off prodigious distances in an era when kicking into touch on the full was not only permitted but where teams like New Zealand, with strong forward bases, used it as a tactical ploy.

Clarke broke the hearts of opponents with the power of his boot. If he wasn't landing goals—and anything within 60 metres was

within his range—he was raking off massive amounts of territory with touchfinders. He once landed a penalty goal in a representative match at Te Kuiti from 84 yards (about 76 metres). On another occasion, in a test match in South Africa, a clearing kick just out from his own goal-line went into touch deep inside the opposition 22.

Probably no single match encapsulates the amazing match-winning capabilities of Clarke more than the second test of the 1960 Springbok series at Bloemfontein. Five minutes from time the South Africans were ahead 11–3, having won the opening international decisively. With five minutes remaining, Clarke kicked a booming penalty goal from just short of his own 10-metre line, and into a slight breeze!

A few minutes later winger Frank McMullen was across for a try, wide out, after latching on to a beautifully-judged grubber kick by Kevin Laidlaw. Clarke was always confident he would land the conversion to make the score 11–11. 'It might sound big-headed,' he said later, 'but after you've played a lot of rugby, you know when you can land a goal. Your kicking is really just an extension of your play. That day I was confident in everything I did.'

Clarke, who was a sufficiently talented fast bowler to represent Auckland at cricket, accumulated 1851 points as an All Black, a record which survived more than a quarter of a century till Grant Fox began peppering the posts.

Clarke has lived in South Africa since 1977. The sign on the gate of his Johannesburg home says 'Kia Ora'.

That's what brothers are for! Ian Clarke steadies the ball for one of brother Don's booming kicks on his test debut against the Springboks at Lancaster Park in 1956.

	Period	Games	Tries	Conv	Pen	DG	Mark	Points
STATISTICS								
Tests	56-64	31	2	33	38	5	2	207
NZ	56-64	89	8	173	120	15	2	781
Total	51-64	207	22	365	318	28	2	1851

MAURICE BROWNLIE

A man of great courage and strength, he was a rugby colossus in the 1920s

No more graphic illustration of the opportunities available to young rugby players of today can be given than by comparing the international careers of two of our greatest All Blacks—Maurice Brownlie and Jeff Wilson.

Of the 61 games that Brownlie—an awesomely powerful loose forward who operated in the 1920s—played for his country, only eight were test matches. Match that with the record of the multi-talented Wilson whose 52 appearances for the All Blacks up to 1999 embraced 42 tests.

How Brownlie would have relished the modern, professional game with its ceaseless action. The Carisbrook fans cherish opportunities to cheer on Goldie whether he's wearing the blue and gold of Otago or the black of New Zealand. But poor Brownlie, a player of legendary status, never got to play a test within his own country. Yet his international career extended from 1922 to 1928—incredibly there were no home tests in that seven-year span. There were All Black outings but the NZRFU refused to grant international status to the almost annual fixtures against New South Wales (prior to the first Australian team being fielded in 1929). Although the Australian Rugby Union finally relented in 1999 and conferred test status on the New South Wales players who took the field against the All Blacks prior to 1929, the NZRFU has so far not been so magnanimous.

Which leaves Brownlie with those eight test appearances, four of which were on the Invincibles' unbeaten tour of the UK and France in 1924–5 and four, as All Black captain, in South Africa in 1928. Just eight tests—a modern international can chalk up that many in a season!

Brownlie was a colossus, the Colin Meads of his day. Like Meads, he wasn't a great leaper in the lineout but in almost every other respect he was the Pinetree of the twenties, possessed of ball-handling skills and pace but above all courage and strength. Meads starred in a television advertisement in the eighties, carrying massive tanalised fence posts up the slopes of his farm. Legend has it that Brownlie managed such journeys with a sheep under each arm.

He won acclaim as the best forward in the world for his deeds on the Invincibles tour, his pinnacle achieved in the English international at Twickenham after his brother Cyril was ordered off in the opening moments. He gave more than 100 per cent that afternoon. He played for himself and his brother, scoring an unforgettable try through sheer determination as he blasted English defenders aside. He had Jim Parker in support but never considered passing. 'Jim, I wouldn't have passed the ball for £100,' he told his colleague later.

His All Black career finished with the 1928 tour of South Africa. Despite almost insurmountable difficulties, his team squared the series, Brownlie later asserting the All Blacks would have triumphed if they had taken Bert Cooke, who was unavailable, and George Nepia, who couldn't tour because he was a Maori.

Brownlie, who played in 25 of the 32 matches on the Invincibles tour, towers over his opponent at Gloucester.

Above: *Brownlie captained the All Blacks to South Africa in 1928. Here he comes off the scrum as the Springbok halfback Pierre de Villiers dive-passes in the first test at Durban.*

Right: *Typical Maurice Brownlie, leading from the front during the 1924–25 All Blacks' match against Swansea at St Helen's. Brownlie scored a try as his team won 39–3.*

	Period	Games	Tries	Conv	Points
STATISTICS					
Tests	24-28	8	2	-	6
NZ	22-28	61	21	-	63
Total	21-30	119	54	12	186

GRANT FOX

No one prepared for a game more diligently than Foxy,
master goal-kicker and strategist

The public remember Grant Fox as a prolific-scoring goal-kicker but his teammates remember him as an astute tactician.

No one prepared for a match more diligently than Fox. As far back as his days with the Auckland Grammar School first XV when his coach was Graham Henry, Fox would compile a schedule of moves, photocopy them and distribute them to every member of the squad.

'That was Foxy's way,' recalls Henry. 'He had an intuitive feeling for the game and had strategies prepared to cover every eventuality. He had a remarkable influence on every team he represented, from schoolboy level right through to the All Blacks. Foxy's teams were always tactically aware and more often than not were successful.'

Of course, if the strategies that Fox and coaches like Henry devised didn't automatically bring success, his deadly accurate right boot was there to compensate. In a career spanning 12 seasons at first-class level, Fox scored a staggering 4106 points from 301 games, at an astonishing average of 13.6 points per game.

Having learnt to goal-kick 'barefoot' on the family farm at Waotu near Putaruru, Fox zealously preserved his right to take kicks at goal. 'Right from the start I enjoyed the craft,' he says. 'My philosophy as a kid was that if I was the best goal-kicker, they would have to play me.'

That attitude never changed. He was once asked to share the goal-kicking duties for Auckland with Greg Cooper. When David Kirk, the Auckland captain, announced he was making the change, Fox spat the dummy. 'I told him, "I do the goal-kicking in this

team!" David didn't change his mind and I later received a dressing down from the coach [John Hart].'

Fox has been eternally grateful that the Lions tour of 1971 promoted the round the corner style of goal-kicking. Until then, everyone it seemed, including young Fox, had toe-kicked. 'It fascinated me,' says Fox. 'Their style impacted on me and I began practising their way. I never did another toe-kick.'

After making his mark as a schoolboy, Fox bounded into the Auckland team in 1982 as a 19-year-old novice. He survived a couple of shaky early performances to command the No. 10 jersey for more than a decade, extending the union's individual point-scoring record from 419 to 2746!

He says the secret to successful goal-kicking lies in technical efficiency and practice routines. 'I see kickers focusing on deep breathing and shaking of the hands. Those things help relax you but if you're not technically correct, they won't get the ball between the posts.'

Fox was an invincible All Black for six seasons, completing 46 matches (including 24 tests) in the black jersey before experiencing defeat. His first reversal came against the Wallabies at Athletic Park in 1990. A far more shattering loss occurred in the World Cup semi-final against the Wallabies in Dublin 14 months later.

Carrying a deep-seated abdominal injury at the time, Fox seriously considered retirement, but new coach Laurie Mains coaxed him back and he contributed massively to a famous test win over the Springboks at Ellis Park and a thrilling series victory over the Lions in 1993. In the last of his 46 tests, against Western Samoa, he kicked seven penalty goals, a New Zealand record.

Grant Fox, for whom goal-kicking became an art form, amassed
2746 points for Auckland and 1067 for the All Blacks.

STATISTICS							
	Period	Games	Tries	Conv	Pen	DG	Points
Tests	85-93	46	1	118	128	7	645
NZ	84-93	78	2	225	192	11	1067
Total	82-93	303	29	901	683	47	4112

KEVIN SKINNER

*Because of one test in 1956
a champion scrummager is remembered as a pugilist*

The great misfortune for Kevin Skinner, one of the toughest and best props ever to pull on the All Black jersey, is that by agreeing in 1956 to come out of retirement and help his country finally overcome the Springbok bogey, he has been largely remembered for his boxing prowess.

Thanks to the solidity Skinner, then 28, brought to the All Black front row, New Zealand, in danger of losing its grip on the series because of the South Africans' scrummaging might, was able to complete a famous series triumph.

But a lot of observers, particularly South Africans who were sore at losing the series, identified Skinner's 'flying fists' more than his scrummaging might as the reason the series turned around so dramatically.

It's true Skinner was a former New Zealand heavyweight boxing champion. It's also true he threw some punches in his recall match at Lancaster Park. But it's not true that his sole objective in that sensational third test was to knock the living daylights out of Springbok props Chris Koch and Jaap Bekker, who'd bent and buckled their opponents at Dunedin and Wellington.

Skinner says there were only a handful of punches thrown. 'What had to change,' says Skinner, 'was our attitude. Our guys were allowing themselves to be intimidated. The Springboks were resorting to gamesmanship and we'd been letting them get away with it.

'I resolved that if the referee wouldn't control their cheating, I would. The first time Chris Koch advanced on to our side of the lineout, I warned him. "That'll be the last time you do that, Chris," I told him. Next lineout, he came through again. So I hit him.

'My attitude was that if there's going to be a donnybrook, let's sort it out here in front of the referee—he's going to warn before he sends anyone off. Play settled down and the South Africans didn't come through the lineout again.'

That was Punch No. 1. Punch No. 2 came early in the second half after Skinner had swapped sides in the front row to give Ian Clarke a break after 40 torrid minutes marking Bekker.

'Bekker liked to throw his weight about and work on you. Straightaway, he started trying to "pop" me, dropping his shoulder and generally making a nuisance of himself. So I hit him. It led to a scuffle which was soon sorted out—and that was that.'

Skinner is emphatic that those were the only two incidents in that third test. 'From what has been written since,' he says, 'you would think the fighting lasted for the entire 80 minutes!'

Irked by events in Christchurch, the Springboks plainly set out to 'get' Skinner and it is obvious that the boot in the back, which put Tiny White out of the fourth test, was intended for Skinner.

Skinner had earlier made 18 consecutive test appearances by the time of his first retirement and been a key member of the crack Otago Ranfurly Shield side of the late forties, as well as captaining his country against Australia in 1952. During the South African tour of 1949 he completed one of the most powerful and effective front rows ever to represent the All Blacks, along with hooker Has Catley and Johnny Simpson.

It's Jaap Bekker, not Kevin Skinner, who's getting a talking-to from referee Bill Fright at Lancaster Park in 1956.

	Period	Games	Tries	Points
STATISTICS				
Tests	49-56	20	1	3
NZ	49-56	63	3	9
Total	47-56	134	6	18

JONAH LOMU

*From a humble background to an
international sporting icon—that's Jonah the Giant*

Almost 1000 New Zealanders have worn the famous black jersey in the 115 years since the first All Black team was fielded. But none has made a greater impact on the world sporting scene than Jonah Lomu.

He has become an international sporting icon, largely as a result of an astonishing 80 minutes of rampaging action at Cape Town during the 1995 Rugby World Cup, when he ran around, through and over the hapless English.

Since that dramatic afternoon when Jonah the Giant, at his unstoppable best, claimed four tries as the All Blacks progressed to the World Cup final, Lomu-mania has been rife. He is now relentlessly hounded by the media and fans mob him for autographs wherever he goes, while developments in his love-life and health are instant front page items. After early contracts with international corporates McDonalds and Reebok, he signed a long-term deal with adidas in 1999 purportedly worth millions of dollars.

Not bad for a boy from South Auckland who grew up on the wrong side of the tracks and was on detention within two hours of starting college. Having lived on the idyllic Tongan island of Ha'apai—where he became known as The Water Rat—until he was seven, Lomu's most impressionable years were in the concrete jungle of South Auckland. He had an uncle and a close friend stabbed to death in revenge attacks by ethnic groups. 'There was a lot of violence,' says Lomu. 'When I was attending intermediate school, if you didn't know how to fight, you got beaten up. Fortunately, I had size on my side.'

Being sent to Wesley College at Pukekohe was his salvation,

although only after a torrid beginning. On his first morning he found himself on detention after he had attacked a seventh former who'd abused him. Principal Chris Grinter—who had been a successful coach of the New Zealand schools rugby team—immediately identified an anger problem and so set up a punching bag in the school's gymnasium. 'Whenever you feel angry,' he told Lomu, 'you let yourself into the gym and take it out on the punching bag instead of your schoolmates.'

Thanks to Wesley's principal and the people who would guide his destiny in rugby, he entirely eliminated anger from his personality, transferring that energy from negatives into positives to help him become a rugby player of exceptional talent and impact. In rapid succession he progressed from the New Zealand schools team, where he startled opponents with his powerful charges from the No. 8 position, to the New Zealand sevens team, wowing fans at Hong Kong with his unrivalled blend of pace and power. From there, it was a straight course, becoming the youngest All Black test player (against France in 1994) at 19 years and 45 days.

In the unfamiliar position of wing, he had his defensive frailties exposed by the French, but 12 months later, more confident and mature, he was unleashed at the World Cup, inflicting unbelievable damage on the UK teams. It was there that he earned his reputation, and notwithstanding occasional lapses of form—including a debilitating liver disease that jeopardised his sporting future—he has emerged as the most instantly recognisable rugby player in the world today.

*Jonah Lomu in action against the Wallabies in 1995,
the year in which he exploded onto the international scene.*

Lomu has reserved his finest rugby for two World Cups—South Africa in 1995 and Wales four years later. His four tries against England in '95 and his two against France in '99 (both at the semi-final stage) represented attacking qualities of the highest order.

STATISTICS

	Period	Games	Tries	Points
Tests	94-99	38	25	125
NZ	94-99	48	31	155
Total	94-99	122	85	425

ZINZAN BROOKE

Nothing was impossible for the multi-talented and incredibly competitive kid from Warkworth

You need go no further than Graham Henry if you're seeking a testimonial for Zinzan Brooke. Together as coach and captain they guided the Auckland NPC team and the Auckland Blues Super 12 teams to greatness.

'He was a player of immense vision who could do things no others could,' says Henry. 'There's never been anyone who led more by example. He possessed a big defence, could run with the backs, scored an astonishing number of tries, organised everyone else and, if all else failed, could drop-kick goals! He was at the peak of his powers through 1996 and early 1997.'

The lowering of standards in the Auckland Blues and All Black teams was all too apparent to New Zealand rugby followers after Brooke packed his rugby gear and headed for London to join the Harlequins club at the conclusion of the 1998 season.

Freakish is not a word applicable to many rugby players but it was certainly appropriate to Brooke. Nothing was ever impossible while you had the multi-talented Aucklander on your side.

He will be remembered for the incredible number of tries he scored as a No. 8 (35 in two seasons with Auckland), his audaciousness in firing giant passes acrossfield to launch attacks, the 'cheeky' tap try he scored against the Springboks at Ellis Park in 1992 and the valuable dropped goals he produced in tests against England and South Africa.

The first of those amazing drop-kicks was in the World Cup semi-final against England at Newlands from 45 metres out. 'Knowing how competitive he is,' commented a teammate afterwards, 'the

only surprise is he didn't use his left foot!'

His other legendary 'pot' helped secure the All Blacks' first series victory on South African soil at Pretoria in 1996. Brooke had experienced intense disappointment in South Africa the previous year when the Springboks nosed out his team in the World Cup final. Now he was determined to gain revenge.

Fourteen months on the All Blacks were leading the Springboks 30–26 with about five minutes to play, the players close to exhaustion.

When the All Blacks secured good ruck ball on the Springbok 22, Brooke was in position behind halfback Justin Marshall and drop-kicked the goal. 'It was the obvious thing to do,' he said later.

It helped make 1996 the season of seasons for Brooke. In addition to that famous series win in South Africa, he shared in the Blues' Super 12 triumph, Auckland's Ranfurly Shield and NPC victories, the All Blacks' Tri-nations and Bledisloe Cup successes and his club team Auckland Marist's Gallaher Shield win.

Surprisingly, he took a long time to secure a regular slot at international level, initially because of Buck Shelford's presence at No. 8 and then because the selectors for a time preferred Arran Pene. Shelford would write in the foreword to Brooke's autobiography that the sadness of his career was that New Zealand audiences saw too little of the genius of the player at top level.

Not till he was 29 did he become a test regular. But what an impact he would make after that. He would finish with 43 tries for New Zealand and 46 for Auckland.

Zinzan Brooke scored 43 tries for the All Blacks. Here's one of the most valuable—against the Springboks at Pretoria in 1996, helping his team to its historic series win.

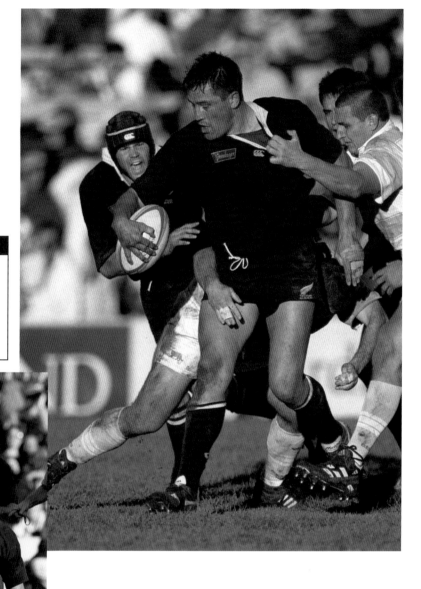

STATISTICS

	Period	Games	Tries	Conv	DG	Points
Tests	87-97	58	17	-	3	89
NZ	87-97	100	43	-	3	195
Total	85-97	311	161	1	3	700

*The multi-talented Zinzan Brooke contributed massively
to the Auckland and New Zealand sides he represented.
He was a leader, a deadly tackler, a champion scorer of
tries, an innovator and he could goal-kick and drop goals.*

BRUCE ROBERTSON

Luxury for a winger in the 1970s was operating outside BJ—the consummate centre

Physiotherapists would not be formally involved with touring rugby teams until 1978, so that when the All Blacks toured the UK and France in 1972–3 they were in the hands of local medics wherever they happened to be.

That proved disastrous for Bruce Robertson, a 20-year-old of unlimited potential in his first year as an international player. Initially sidelined with a broken thumb, Robertson damaged a hamstring when he stepped in a pot-hole while training at Porthcawl in Wales.

A team physio would undoubtedly have repaired the damage in a couple of weeks but the bewildered young centre was shunted from physio to doctor to physio to quack to physio to rubber-downer as the All Blacks journeyed along on their 32-match tour. His hamstrings never came right. He continued to play despite the frustrations and the ignorance of local medical people.

Against Scotland at Murrayfield he sought to come off at half-time, both hamstrings hurting and preventing him from running at more than three-quarter pace. But the duty doctor wouldn't give him a clearance to leave the field. The doctor told him he would have to tear the muscle completely before he could go off. 'I had the last laugh,' says Robertson. 'I could still sidestep and kick and I managed to slip a wee grubber kick through for Grant Batty to score. It's just as well I didn't have to chase any speedsters like Andy Irvine.'

Such was the damage caused to Robertson's hamstring muscles on that tour he claims it was a full three years before he could stretch out properly and run with complete freedom.

Fortunately for New Zealand rugby, the classical centre would do plenty of stretching out for the remainder of his career to create try-scoring opportunities for the country's leading wingers. Operating outside him, Bryan Williams, Grant Batty and Stu Wilson—All Blacks of outstanding calibre—collectively ran in more than 150 tries in the black jersey.

Williams would say of Robertson that he 'quickly came to appreciate the luxury benefits of playing outside such a swift and talented centre' while Batty branded him 'the No. 1 centre in the world for as long as I was in test rugby'.

Robertson had a meteoric rise to stardom in 1971, bounding from the Ardmore senior club team, where he was operating as a fullback, into the Counties representative side, where coach Barry Bracewell helped mould his career. It was all very bewildering for the trainee teacher who'd grown up in Hastings and who, at the start of 1971, thought his sporting future lay in cricket.

He was fast-forwarded into the All Blacks in 1972, making an instant impact and embarking on a distinguished career that would extend for nine years. In 1980 he led the All Blacks onto Cardiff Arms Park against Wales in celebration of his 100th appearance.

He scored 32 tries for the All Blacks but it was the tries he created for others for which he is remembered. There was no finer sight than Robertson, his long fair hair streaming behind him, accelerating into a gap.

Rugby remains his passion. For many years the Auckland Rugby Union's coaching director, he is now the union's rugby manager.

Bruce Robertson has Gareth Evans perplexed as he attacks against the British Lions at Carisbrook in 1977.

38

IAN KIRKPATRICK

*The Ngatapa farmer dazzled audiences worldwide
with his devastating running*

All Black selectors are understanding and compassionate these days. If they're about to axe an established international, the news is relayed to him personally before the team announcement is made public.

It wasn't that way in the 1970s. If you doubt that, just ask Ian Kirkpatrick, the magnificently athletic Poverty Bay flanker who scored 115 tries in a celebrated career and who was often referred to as the best player in the world.

Kirkpatrick was unfortunate enough to be captain of the 1972–3 All Blacks to the UK and France—unfortunate because the manager Ernie Todd was (unbeknown at the time) terminally ill and struggling to adequately fulfil his duties. It was the series when controversial prop Keith Murdoch was sent home for striking a security guard after the Welsh international and the team was condemned for its indifferent record—five losses and two draws from 32 games—and poor public image.

Kirkpatrick, 25 at the time, would be the big loser. Although he retained his leadership through 1973, further muddled All Black performances would lead to him becoming the first player to be stripped of the captaincy.

No one warned him of what was coming. In the dank atmosphere of the Athletic Park social room in May 1974, he listened to the team being announced for the tour of Australia. He was retained as a player but yielded the captaincy to Andy Leslie. 'It was a disappointment,' he admits, 'but I wasn't too surprised. Some of the papers had been hinting at a change and after the results of the previous two years, I suppose someone had to go.'

Kirkpatrick, great sportsman that he was, gave his unqualified backing to Leslie and went on to produce some of his finest rugby over the next three seasons. But by 1977 the selectors decided they no longer required the services of the mighty farmer from Ngatapa. A quick phone call to say 'Thanks Kirky' would have been nice. Instead, he heard the announcement of the team to tour France while on the Poverty Bay team bus. Kirky, one of New Zealand's greatest players, deserved better.

Unknown nationally, he was plucked from the New Zealand under-23 team and catapulted into Fred Allen's All Blacks for the 1967 tour of Europe, making such rapid progress that he displaced Kel Tremain for the French international, an unthinkable happening. He would eventually cement a place in the test line-up at Tremain's expense, going on to dazzle audiences worldwide with his devastating running with the ball. Some of the tries he scored—and there were 50 of them for his country—rank among the game's most memorable. One stands out in particular—a dazzling 60-metre gallop against the 1971 British Lions at Lancaster Park.

Kirkpatrick, an exceedingly modest individual, can reflect on a succession of outstanding achievements. He captained both the North and South Islands as well as his country; he helped Canterbury win the Ranfurly Shield from Hawkes Bay; he created test records for most test tries and most consecutive test appearances (which have since been eclipsed); he represented New Zealand at polo and was awarded the MBE. He was also the manager of the infamous Cavaliers on their tour of South Africa in 1986.

*When Irish flyhalf Barry McGann blocked his way, Kirkpatrick took the most expedient route
to the goal-line at Athletic Park in 1976—over the top!*

Ian Kirkpatrick, an individual who could impose himself on a game, scored 50 tries for the All Blacks. Here's one of the most valuable against England at Twickenham in 1973.

STATISTICS

	Period	Games	Tries	Points
Tests	67-77	39	16	57
NZ	67-77	113	50	180
Total	66-79	285	114	406

Above: *The dynamic attacking qualities of Kirkpatrick evident here against South West Selection at Tarbes at the tail-end of the long, demanding tour of the UK and France in 1972–73.*

GEORGE NEPIA

The greatest hero of all from the Invincibles tour was the teenager from Nuhaka

What were the New Zealand selectors thinking of by naming just one fullback for a 32-match tour of the UK, France and British Columbia in 1924? That was crazy enough in itself, but the player they chose was only 19 and inexperienced in the position.

It is not recorded whether the rugby correspondents of the time questioned the sanity of the selectors in taking such a gamble—although one writer dared to suggest this was the feeblest All Black team despatched from these shores. Eight months later that team was being hailed as the Invincibles, having registered 32 consecutive victories.

And the greatest hero of all was the teenager from Nuhaka on the East Coast. George Nepia who, staggeringly for someone who had concentrated on five-eighth play until a few weeks before the touring party was selected, had operated at fullback in every single game.

Nepia, who was furiously asking questions of fullbacks in the days before his All Black debut, performed as if he were born to the position. *Wisden's Rugby Almanack* named him one of its five players of the year while Wavell Wakefield, the England captain, later wrote that 'his perfect catching of the ball, his kicking and his amazing power of breaking up a forward rush by whipping the ball off the ground and charging backwards through oncoming forwards marked him out as a player of a generation'.

Nepia may never have become the famous fullback he did had he not defied his father's plans for his schooling. He had been despatched by train to the renowned Maori school Te Aute College, where his fees had been paid. Instead, on impulse, George exited

the train at Hastings and accompanied his friends to the Maori Agricultural College, a Mormon establishment.

It seems inconceivable that he was not bundled off down the line but a teacher at the school, Elder Moser, an American, was impressed with his sporting potential and undertook to fund his education. Furthermore, he taught Nepia the fundamentals of gridiron tackling where the tackler leaves his feet and hits the ball carrier with his shoulders. His instruction would convert Nepia into a tackler without peer.

Nepia, ever modest, downplayed his achievements on the Invincibles tour, claiming they were such a great team they would have won many of their contests without a fullback!

A key member of the crack Hawkes Bay Ranfurly Shield team of the 1920s, Nepia bowed out as an All Black against Great Britain in 1930, having been ineligible to tour South Africa in 1928 because Maoris were not welcome. When he missed All Black selection in 1935, he switched codes, playing club league in England and representing the Kiwis in 1937.

Reinstated to rugby during the war years, he made a couple of first-class appearances for East Coast in 1947 at the not inconsiderable age of 42.

Nepia was christened simply George but, at the suggestion of a friend, he adopted the middle initials M. H. which stayed with him throughout his career. In 1986, a few months before he died, he was the subject of the television programme *This Is Your Life*. It was watched by 1.2 million New Zealanders, more than a third of the population.

Fullbacks were essentially defenders in the 1920s but George Nepia demonstrates that he could attack effectively too—against Wales at Swansea, a test the tourists won 19–0.

KEL TREMAIN

*The irrepressible flanker from Hawkes Bay
who never stopped scoring tries*

Hawkes Bay has enjoyed two classic Ranfurly Shield tenures—one in the 1920s and the other in the 1960s. Both times inspiration was provided by a dynamic loose forward.

In the twenties it was Maurice Brownlie, the outstanding forward of his time. Forty years on, the individual who guided the Hawkeye guys to greatness was Kel Tremain, an irrepressible player with an astonishing capacity for scoring tries.

He was remarkably swift and agile for someone so big and weighed more than 100 kilograms for most of his career, exceptional for a flanker in the sixties. In sight of the goal-line he was virtually unstoppable and scored 136 tries in his distinguished career. It was a record for a New Zealand forward until the equally exceptional Zinzan Brooke came along.

A couple of his tries have passed into rugby folklore. One of the most important was the match-winner against France in the hurricane at Wellington in 1961 when he plucked the ball off fullback Pierre Lacaze's boot as he went to kick for touch. On another occasion he burrowed under the entire North Auckland pack in the dying moments to save the Shield for his beloved Hawkes Bay team. The Northlanders insisted he'd grounded the ball short of the goalline. Tremain himself didn't know but the referee awarded the try— and that was all that mattered.

Tremain broke into the All Blacks in 1959 and became a permanent fixture on the side of the scrum for almost an entire decade. He originally believed that if he was to play for his country it would be as a lock. He can thank Bob Stuart, Canterbury's coach in 1958,

for sorting him out on that one. 'I was annoyed that Bob made me operate as a breakaway at my first representative practice,' said Tremain. 'I spoke to him afterwards and told him I was trying to become an All Black as a lock, that flankers were two a penny and that the secret to a long life in the All Blacks was to get there as a lock.'

'If you want to be a lock,' Stuart replied, 'don't bother coming back to another training session!'

Tremain became a great mate of Colin Meads. During the series in South Africa in 1960 they were having problems with Martin Pelser, one of the toughest, most rugged opponents either of them ever encountered. 'Pinetree and I agreed that in the first test one of us would jump while the other "fixed" Pelser. Some theory that turned out to be. He floored both of us and got the lineout ball!'

While New Zealanders generally remember Tremain as a great All Black, Hawkes Bay fans unquestionably recall the mighty flanker for his heroics during the three years the Bay held the Shield after taking it from Waikato in 1966.

Far from fading into oblivion after retiring, Tremain, ever passionate for rugby, put an immense amount back into the game, serving as Hawkes Bay chairman and then NZRFU councillor. He was tipped as a future chairman but in 1992, only a month after managing the New Zealand Sevens team to Hong Kong, he died of lung cancer complicated by severe pneumonia. He was just 54. The day he died all club players in Hawkes Bay stood for a minute in silence as a tribute to the great man.

---

*Tremain and Springbok halfback Nelie Smith resort to soccer
skills on the treacherous surface of Carisbrook during the 1965 test series.*

N.Z. Rugby Football Union

No. 2B UNCOVERED STAND
SOUTH-WEST CORNER

ATHLETIC PARK
SOUTH AFRICA v. NEW ZEALAND

SATURDAY, 31st JULY, 1965

464   25/-   Secretary, N.Z.R.F.U.

Reserved Seat

Holder of Ticket to be admitted at either
South End, Adelaide Road or South End,
Rintoul Street Entrance.

Above: *Tremain scored one of
his most valuable tries in the test
between South Africa and New
Zealand at Athletic Park in 1965,
securing a 6–3 win for the All
Blacks at the start of the series.
He also scored tries in the second
and third tests.*

48

Kel Tremain scored a whopping 136 tries in his career, a remarkable number for such a big, powerful forward. Here's one of them in a trial match.

STATISTICS

	Period	Games	Tries	Mark	Points
Tests	59-68	38	9	-	27
NZ	59-68	86	36	-	108
Total	57-70	268	136	1	411

Left: Hawkes Bay was overcome with Shield fever in the 1960s, in no small measure thanks to the dynamic qualities of the team's captain Kel Tremain. Here he is chaired off McLean Park, Napier, near the end of his career.

BOB SCOTT

*The miracle performer who had difficulty
wrapping up his celebrated career*

Bob Scott always thought he knew the most appropriate time to retire. But others didn't. And so the fullback who many rate the greatest ever—greater even than George Nepia—made two notable comebacks, and almost a third, before finally crying enough.

The first curtain-down on Scott's celebrated career came after the 1951 season when, at the age of 30, he decided to devote himself to his family and the textile business he'd established in Ponsonby. But the following winter he was lured back into action late in the season by the chairman of the Auckland union, Tom Pearce. Scott performed indifferently, didn't enjoy his rugby particularly and promptly went back into retirement.

Between seasons, and following a sparkling end-of-season performance for the Barbarians, he was approached by two NZRFU officials who pleaded with him to make himself available for the All Black tour of the UK and France scheduled for 1953–54.

'It wasn't so much a request as a demand,' recalls Scott. 'I realised I was opening myself to criticism having retired twice, but I felt I still had plenty of rugby in me. So I made the decision to go for it. It's not a decision I have ever regretted.'

Scott was a quality performer throughout the All Black tour which, with additional outings in Canada and America on the way home, stretched to 36 matches. A favourite target of autograph hunters, he influenced the course of countless matches, not only through his goal-kicking and drop-kicking skills but also his deft ability to elude tacklers and create attacking opportunities for his team.

It was claimed he 'performed miracles' in the 19–5 win over the Barbarians at Cardiff after which he was chaired from the field. Another brilliant performance was against England in brutal conditions at Twickenham. After this game, the *Times* correspondent O. L. Owen described the All Blacks as 'a great team—and Scott'. It was no wonder he earned the nickname of 'The Master'.

Satisfied that he'd served his country well, Scott retired, finally he thought. Yet such was his genius that when the Springboks toured in 1956 and he was 35, national administrators tried to lure him back into action once more. Although he was still playing club rugby of the highest quality, he declined.

Rugby claimed Scott only because the NZRFU declared an amnesty on league players during the war. Until then, Scott, who'd had a challenging childhood—his father eking out an existence on the railways in a desolate part of the King Country—had played only league.

He would first make his mark as a rugby player with the Kiwis following the war, becoming the All Black fullback when international fixtures were resumed in 1946.

Although he retains the fondest memories of his times in the black jersey, Scott frowns when he recalls the 1949 tour of South Africa. There the All Blacks suffered a humiliating whitewash even though they outscored the Springboks in tries. 'I suffered extreme depression on that tour,' says Scott who felt he could have swung the outcome had he produced his finest goal-kicking form.

Bob Scott starts a match in South Africa in 1949. He admits to suffering 'extreme depression' over events on that tour.

	Period	Games	Tries	Conv	Pen	DG	Points
Tests	46-54	17	-	16	12	2	74
NZ	46-54	52	1	58	33	8	242
Total	42-61	152	7	246	93	16	840

STATISTICS

BRYAN WILLIAMS

The teenage 'coloured boy' launched a spectacular international career in South Africa

Bryan Williams, or Beegee as he is popularly known in the rugby world, has made more appearances for the All Blacks than any other back, 113 in total. The number should have been 114 and his international debut should have been in Perth, not at Bethlehem in South Africa in 1970, but for an embarrassing injury sustained back in Auckland.

The 19-year-old was understandably reticent about divulging details of his damaged quadricep at the time because it happened when he tumbled in Auckland's Albert Park while on a university pub crawl.

'It wasn't the sort of announcement a teenager about to embark on the trip of a lifetime as an All Black wanted to make public,' says Williams. 'I'd had the muscle repaired after damaging it in training and my fall in the park undid all the good work.'

The rugby fans of Perth were thus denied the spectacle of Williams in action but it wouldn't be long before South African enthusiasts were raving about the skills of the young Samoan winger.

Williams was creating history when he stepped off the plane in Johannesburg because he was one of the first four 'non-white' sportsmen accepted by the South African Government, which still operated under the apartheid policy. No Maori or Polynesians had been included in the All Black teams of 1928, 1949 or 1960. Beegee was helping break down the barriers, along with teammates Sid Going, Blair Furlong and Buff Milner, all of Maori descent.

He would instantly become the darling of the coloured population as he dazzled opponents with his rare blend of pace, power and sidestepping skills. Unfortunately, their enthusiasm would lead to

violence after the game at Kimberley. Having invaded the field after the final whistle, the coloureds hoisted him onto their shoulders, a gesture which didn't trouble Williams. But suddenly a number of whites, who had been drinking, attacked the coloureds, the police became involved and a full-scale riot ensued. It was an ugly reminder of the tensions that existed under the apartheid system.

Such was his popularity, he received more than 1000 letters from South Africans after his return home.

The reputation Williams established on that tour would remain with him throughout his exciting and colourful career. He would go on to score 66 tries for his country, a figure bettered only by John Kirwan, and he also proved a valuable goal-kicker, specialising in long-range efforts.

Notwithstanding a terrible hip injury suffered at Toulouse in 1977 that threatened his entire sporting career, he would remain a first-choice All Black winger until 1978. And he would play a remarkable 15 seasons with Auckland, rounding out his career as a fullback. He was named the New Zealand rugby player of the decade in 1980.

Gerald Davies, the great Welsh and Lions player, singled him out as his most difficult opponent because 'he was stockily built and very fast with a devastating sidestep off his left foot'.

Williams has continued to embrace rugby since his retirement. As a coach he guided his Ponsonby club to Gallaher Shield honours and assisted Maurice Trapp through an astonishingly successful era with Auckland (86 victories from 90 matches). He then became coach of Manu Samoa and in 2000 is assisting Graham Mourie with the preparation of the Hurricanes Super 12 team.

Beegee Williams dives across for a try against Paul Ross' XV at Bethlehem on the South Africa tour of 1970. He went on to score 66 tries for his country.

	Period	Games	Tries	Conv	Pen	DG	Points
STATISTICS							
Tests	70-78	38	10	2	9	1	71
NZ	70-78	113	66	22	30	1	401
Total	68-82	269	137	41	77	1	825

MICHAEL JONES

The Samoan loose forward forever amazed fans and opponents, but never on Sundays

Life was a lot less complicated for rugby players in the amateur days of the 1980s. In those blissful times there were no penalties for representing more than one nation. You could turn out for a country a year or two after you'd played test rugby for another. That's what happened to Michael Jones—arguably the greatest loose forward of all time. He made his test debut for Western Samoa against Wales in Apia in 1985 and two years later was representing the All Blacks in spectacular fashion at the first Rugby World Cup.

Jones, who is half Samoan and proud of his heritage, was lured into action at Apia by fellow Auckland representative Peter Fatialofa who would lead the great revival of Samoan rugby. Michael has never forgotten the occasion, not so much for his or the team's performance but because of the manner in which he was introduced to the Head of State by the team's captain Dick Tafua. 'He announced me as Tom Jones,' says Michael. 'Can you believe that? And us playing Wales? I was still laughing about it as the game was about to start.'

The real Tom Jones, a famous entertainer, surely wouldn't have minded being confused with the player who would go on to become a legend in his lifetime. If Fatialofa had identified Michael's exquisite rugby skills, so had John Hart. He would introduce him to his Auckland representative team that same year—Jones responding with a hat-trick of tries on debut—and in 1987 he would push for his involvement in the World Cup squad.

Jones, who would never stop amazing people throughout his illustrious career, scored the first individual try at that first World Cup. He also scored the first try in the second World Cup. The opportunity for an incredible hat-trick was denied him in 1995 when the All Black selectors left him behind because a large percentage of their programme involved Sunday play, and Michael, a committed Christian, never played sport on Sundays. His stand on Sunday sport cost him many, many appearances for Auckland and New Zealand but it never troubled him. His faith sustained him. That same faith brought him through a rugby accident in 1989 so severe that doctors feared he would never play sport again, the injury necessitating the complete reconstruction of his knee.

Jones became the consummate openside flanker, the scourge of opposition backs because of his marvellous athletic ability and animal-like instincts. For much of his career—which in total involved 55 tests and 83 games for Auckland—he starred as an openside flanker. With his pace slightly diminished, he switched to the blindside where he became equally as effective, but only after he'd changed his body shape to meet the physical demands of this different position.

His favourite memories are of winning the inaugural World Cup and sharing in a series win on South African soil for the first time. To create history in South Africa many of the All Blacks pushed themselves to the point of exhaustion, and beyond. 'The Pretoria test [which clinched the series] was probably the most physically sapping game I had ever been involved in. The referee's whistle for full-time was such a sweet sound.'

Michael Jones won a reputation as the greatest loose forward of all time.
Here he demonstrates his talents for Auckland against Queensland in a Super 10 game in 1995.

The young Michael Jones at his athletic best, as a 22-year-old in the World Cup opener against Italy at Eden Park in 1987.

STATISTICS				
Period	Games	Tries	Conv	Points
Tests	87-98	55	13	-	56
NZ	87-98	74	16	-	69
Total	85-99	229	76	2	335

NB Jones also played one test for Samoa

Marvellous Michael had the distinction of scoring the first try at each of the first two World Cups—against Italy in Auckland in 1987 and against England at Twickenham in 1991.

Jones's illustrious representative career, which stretched across 15 seasons, came to a conclusion following Auckland's victory over Wellington in the NPC final in 1999.

The World cup final of 1987 remains among Michael Jones's most treasured moments. He scored a try as New Zealand downed France to claim the world crown.

57

BERT COOKE

The pint-sized midfielder who won over the Prince of Wales

If Don Clarke and Jonah Lomu rate as two of the biggest and most imposing individuals ever to represent the All Blacks, Bert Cooke was probably the lightest.

The midfielder who dazzled audiences in the UK on the Invincibles tour of 1924–25 weighed just eight and a half stone (around 54 kilograms, a veritable jockey's weight and some 74 kilograms lighter than Lomu). According to Sir Terry McLean in his book *New Zealand Rugby Legends*, Cooke swore the doctors of the time to secrecy and persuaded them to publish his weight at 9st 5lb (60 kilograms) which survived—like George Nepia's equally fictitious middle names—throughout his playing career.

The Prince of Wales, who later became King Edward VIII, referred to Cooke as 'Little Rat' in an address he delivered to the British Sportsmen's luncheon in London on that 1924 tour, a function at which the All Blacks were the special guests. When Cooke later asked him why he used that title, the Prince said, 'It's the way you dart at a hole—you are quicker than a rat.'

It was a dubious distinction to be so identified by the Prince of Wales but Cooke certainly deserved to be singled out. He was most definitely unique. Operating mostly at second-five, he was possessed of exceptional acceleration. An English journalist wrote of him in 1924 that he was 'as swift as a hare, as elusive as a shadow; strikes like lightning, flashes with brilliancy'. Fellow 1924 All Black Ces Badeley said of him that while Mark Nicholls and George Nepia

were great players, 'they were orthodox, but Cooke was different—he was instinctive; there was no answer to him, he was unreadable'.

Cooke, who scored 23 tries in his 25 outings for the Invincibles, including two in the test against France, was the fastest in the team over 50 metres—no mean achievement considering the touring party included Jim Parker and Jack Steel, both professional sprinters.

He was particularly adept at chipping the ball ahead and recapturing it. Despite his size, he was enormously courageous and never shied off tackles; indeed, his technique was so good that he consistently lowered players twice his size. It was a boast of his that no player, regardless of his size or skill, could run with his knees jammed together.

He was also a star of the celebrated 1926 Hawkes Bay Ranfurly Shield team, the side that put 77 points on Wairarapa, 58 points on Wellington, 41 on Auckland and successfully took the 'log' on tour, defeating Canterbury in Christchurch.

When the next year he set up business in Masterton, he helped Wairarapa take the Shield from Hawkes Bay, ending a tenure which had stretched back five seasons.

The little genius who was Bert Cooke rounded out his playing career with league, his skills taking him into the New Zealand team for test series against Great Britain and, finally, Australia in 1935, 12 years after his representative rugby debut.

Bert Cooke was the leading try-scorer on the Invincibles' 1924–25 tour of the UK.
Here he runs in one of his 23 three-pointers.

STATISTICS

	Period	Games	Tries	Conv	Pen	DG	Points
Tests	24-30	8	4	-	-	-	12
NZ	24-30	44	38	3	-	-	120
Total	23-32	131	119	27	6	3	441

WAKA NATHAN

The Black Panther took his set-backs on the jaw and never stopped giving his best

Serious injuries are the curse of rugby players when they're touring overseas. Imagine, then, how Waka Nathan felt when he sustained broken jaws on successive All Black tours of the UK and France in the 1960s.

'The first one was frustrating enough,' says Nathan, who became known as the Black Panther for the manner in which he stalked opposition backs, 'but finishing up with a second broken jaw was unbelievable.'

Boasting probably the greatest appetite of any member of the 1963–64 team, Nathan found having his jaw wired frustrating in the extreme. 'All I wanted for breakfast was sausages and eggs,' he says. 'Instead, all I could handle were soups, egg-nogs and jellies.' However, there was a brief respite when he broke the wiring in his excitement during the Scottish international. The jaw had to be re-wired the next morning but not before Nathan had gulped down a satisfying breakfast of solids!

Nathan was told he wouldn't play for a couple of months but managed to convince a doctor in Belfast that the wire had been on for six and a half weeks when it had actually been on only for three weeks! She removed it and an eager Nathan returned to action to star in the French test and the fabulous 36–3 win over the Barbarians. Despite the injury break, he gathered 11 tries on tour, the third-best haul behind wingers Malcolm Dick and Ralph Caulton.

Four years later he would bounce back from another disaster with his jaw to play against the Barbarians again. The special significance of this was that the Barbarians regarded him as such a celebrity they invited him to represent them against the All Blacks,

as Ian Clarke had done in 1964.

'I was prepared to accept the invitation,' says Nathan, 'because no Maori had ever represented the Baabaas. It would have been a great honour for my race. But Fred Allen, our coach, wasn't prepared to release me.' Probably just as well—the All Blacks dropped a lot of passes, before escaping with an 11–6 victory, and the Black Panther could have been lethal pouncing on them!

Nathan won international renown for his powerful running and deadly tackling, although he is probably best remembered within New Zealand for his Ranfurly Shield-saving try for Auckland against Canterbury at Eden Park in 1960. Time was up with Auckland trailing 14–18 when Nathan gathered in a sweet kick through by his old Otahuhu College buddy Mac Herewini and ran round behind the posts for the winning score.

The only time he experienced defeat in 37 outings (which included 14 tests) for the All Blacks was against Newport early in the 1963–64 tour.

Having represented New Zealand Maori in the early sixties and being proud of his ancestry, Nathan was saddened to observe the depths to which Maori rugby had plunged by 1969, the year he retired. Precious few of the nation's leading Maori players were making themselves available for the national team. 'I see a way back to the top for Maori rugby,' said Nathan. 'When it happens, it will be more magnificent than ever.'

Nathan himself would help lead the revival. In the seventies as coach he inspired the comeback, later becoming the Maori representative on the NZRFU.

Waka Nathan in the rare role of lineout jumper, against England at Christchurch in 1963.

60

STATISTICS

	Period	Games	Tries	Points
Tests	62-67	14	4	12
NZ	62-67	37	23	69
Total	59-67	171	55	165

JEFF WILSON

Marvellously talented, Goldie has always been committed to the black jersey

More spectators than you would normally have expected for a schoolboys' rugby international in Sydney turned up at the Football Stadium in 1992. Word had leaked out that there was a player of freakish quality in the New Zealand side.

The fans would not be disappointed, except that the superstar of the evening was not the individual they'd been tipped off about, Jonah Lomu. He was upstaged by a blond-haired, fresh-faced fullback called Jeff Wilson. Even Wilson acknowledges it as probably the most complete performance of his career.

Experienced critics were left gasping at his achievements, the most notable of which was a 75-metre try he scored after crash-tackling the Australian centre Brad Condon. As the ball spilled behind the stunned Condon, Wilson scooped it up, sidestepped two players and sprinted three-quarters of the field to dot down between the uprights.

A penalty goal from halfway and a couple of try-saving tackles were the trimmings on an unforgettable performance which won him the Bronze Boot Trophy awarded to the most constructive player in the test.

He'd won the previous match for New Zealand schools with a wide-angle 40-metre penalty goal in injury time, a success which so delighted Lomu, he hoisted Wilson high in the air as the broken-hearted Irish opponents slumped to the ground.

It was around that time his teammates began calling him Goldie, partly because of his fair hair but mostly because of his golden-boy heroics which would continue to distinguish him throughout his

sporting career.

This is an individual who represented his country at rugby and cricket at 19, scoring a hat-trick of tries (against Scotland) in his test debut and playing a winning innings in a one-day cricket international against Australia in Hamilton.

This is also the player who once scored 66 points, including nine tries, in a match for his Cargill High School first XV in an annual grudge match. Prominent basketball coach Tab Baldwin also considers Wilson good enough to represent his country at that sport as well.

Perhaps, not surprisingly, he had a book written about him, appropriately entitled *The Natural*, before he was 21.

While his onfield exploits continue to delight fans and dismay opponents, and have made him the darling of Carisbrook, history may determine that a brave decision he and fellow Otago player Josh Kronfeld took in 1995 represents his greatest moment. Those two broke the deadlock when it seemed Ross Turnbull's WRC was close to contracting the All Blacks after rugby went professional. Wilson and Kronfeld were the first to sign with the NZRFU, a fatal blow to WRC. 'It was probably the hardest decision of my life,' he says, 'but I wanted to keep wearing the All Black jersey.'

If everything seems rosy for Wilson, he endured a terrible sadness late in 1998 when his father Bill, his manager, confidante and 'best mate', died suddenly, in his forties.

Jeff Wilson has excelled at several sports, representing his country at both rugby and one-day cricket as a 19-year-old.

	STATISTICS					
	Period	Games	Tries	Conv	Pen	DG	Points
Tests	93-99	54	39	1	3	1	209
NZ	93-99	65	45	11	8	1	274
Total	92-99	187	131	74	67	4	1016

There are few more skilful attacking rugby players in the
world than Wilson, as French substitute Stephane Glas
discovers during the 1999 World Cup semi-final at Twickenham.

WILSON WHINERAY

The inspirational leader who became the first All Black to be knighted

Rugby teams worldwide refer to the move where a forward doubling back at a lineout takes the tapdown and surges out into midfield as the 'Willie Away'. It's a potent move and, worked well, frequently leads to tries being scored.

The player after whom the move was named is Wilson Whineray. He's now Sir Wilson, the first All Black to be knighted, but during the 1963–64 tour of the UK, his teammates knew him affectionately as Willie.

And Willie Away was a natural tag for the lethal move that the All Blacks devised—a modification of a tactic employed by the 1961 French team. The move was made for him, for as a durable and surprisingly mobile prop (and a former New Zealand Universities heavyweight boxing champion), he possessed the necessary strength to power upfield from lineouts.

Whineray would be remembered for a lot more than that innovative move. Many regard him as the All Blacks' greatest captain, a true ambassador as well as an inspirational onfield leader. The All Blacks enjoyed some of their greatest triumphs under Whineray, seldom experiencing defeat save for the frustrating series loss in South Africa in 1960.

He would take revenge five years later, leading his country to a 3–1 series victory over Dawie de Villiers' Springboks, an appropriate note, Whineray determined, upon which to retire.

Whineray's early rugby career took some believing. As a farm trainee on a government rural cadetship, he was posted to different regions almost annually, as a result of which he played representative rugby for Wairarapa, Mid-Canterbury, Manawatu, Canterbury and Waikato before finally settling in Auckland, where he represented the blue and whites for seven years.

Having shared in the NZ Universities' upset victory over the Springboks in 1956, Whineray was promoted to the All Blacks for the tour of Australia in 1957. Another young buck new to the international scene then was Colin Meads. They made their test debuts together the same afternoon at the Sydney Cricket Ground—Meads aged 20, Whineray 21. Whineray wouldn't miss a test until 1964, while Meads was still in the All Black pack in 1971!

Although Whineray was the captain when Auckland lifted the Ranfurly Shield off Southland in 1959—his personal plea to each member of his forward pack for the 'supreme effort' 15 minutes from time allowing the challenger to come from behind and win—he would graciously yield the Auckland leadership to Bob Graham because of his All Black commitments.

Yet the 1963–64 All Black tour was the pinnacle of his career as a captain. Of the 36 matches played in the UK, France and Canada, the All Blacks won 34—the Newport game was lost 3–0 and the Scottish international drawn 0–0. Terry McLean wrote of him, 'Highly intelligent, mature beyond his years—a firm but calm leader who commanded unqualified admiration. I would unhesitatingly acclaim him as New Zealand's greatest captain.'

Success followed Sir Wilson long after his rugby career ended. In business, he became chairman of Carter Holt Harvey; in sport, he served on the Eden Park Board of Control, and as chairman of the Hillary Commission and as a life member of the New Zealand Sports Foundation.

Although he played nearly all his international rugby at prop, Whineray had the speed and agility of a loose forward, as he displays here against Australia at Sydney in 1957.
Inset: Wilson Whineray chaired off at Cardiff after the memorable Barbarians game of 1964.

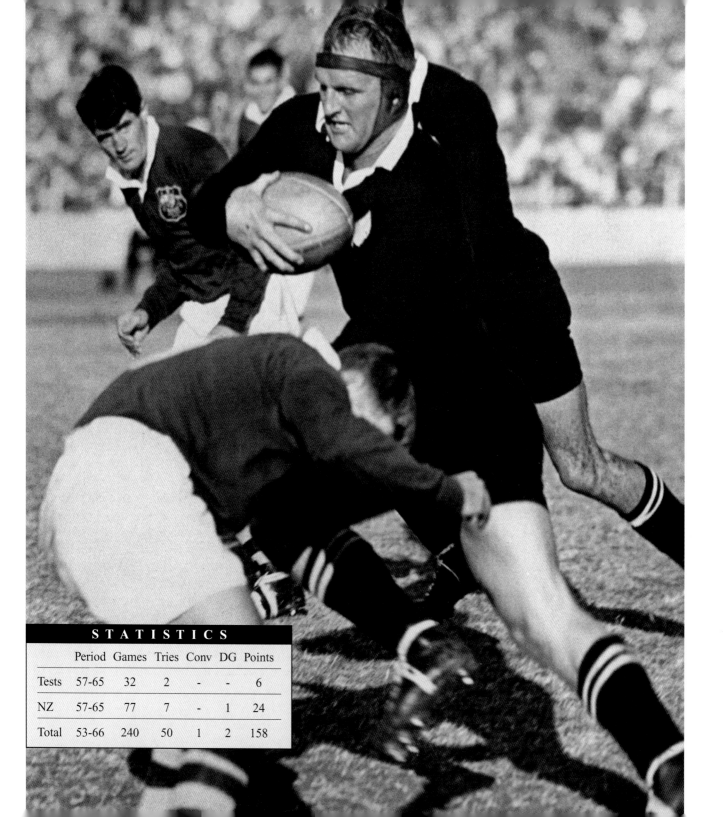

SEAN FITZPATRICK

*Fitzy, the consummate professional
who was determined to become No. 1*

The Irish have a word for it—'bejasus'. It fitted the occasion perfectly. For there at Lansdowne Road in Dublin, on 15 November 1997, were the All Blacks taking the field for an international without Sean Fitzpatrick in the No. 2 jersey.

It was an historic occasion. Apart from that romp against Japan at Bloemfontein during the 1995 Rugby World Cup—bizarre because after Laurie Mains insisted on resting his élite players, the All Blacks accumulated 145 points—this was the first occasion in more than 90 tests, spanning four coaches (Brian Lochore, Alex Wyllie, Laurie Mains and John Hart) and 11 years, that Fitzy wasn't in his beloved No. 2 jersey. Bejasus!

You had to go back to the long-forgotten series against Alan Jones's Wallabies in 1986, a season soured by the Cavaliers' unauthorised tour of South Africa, to locate the previous time New Zealand had fielded a test hooker other than Sean Brian Thomas Fitzpatrick, son of 1950s All Black midfielder Brian Bernard James (popularly known as BBJ) Fitzpatrick.

Over a dozen seasons Fitzpatrick developed from a fresh-faced, enthusiastic, rather loose-tongued hooker into the consummate professional, ultimately rivalling Colin Meads as the greatest All Black ever. Initially considered too loquacious, too ready to bait referees and opponents, to take on the mantle of leadership, Fitzpatrick responded magnificently to the demands of captaincy when it was handed to him by coach Mains in 1992. After a shaky start—his first test speech, following the centenary encounter against a World XV in Christchurch was a losing one—he became an outstanding leader.

Although there would be the occasional set-back thereafter, most disappointingly following the Rugby World Cup final at Ellis Park in 1995, the great majority of Fitzy's after-match speeches throughout his six years as captain featured a winning tone. He won international acclaim for his dynamic and inspiring leadership qualities, a celebrated career coming to an end in 1998 when the serious deterioration of his knee forced retirement.

Fitzpatrick's greatest years as an All Black came after he seriously considered retiring following New Zealand's unsuccessful campaign at the 1991 World Cup. Through the summer that followed, it niggled him that the Wallabies were world champions and Phil Kearns, his great rival, was being dubbed the best hooker in the world. 'That started to grate,' he said. 'I knew I wouldn't rest easily unless I had a crack at claiming that title back.'

The philosophy he applied when he resumed training in 1992 was that he was No. 2, wanting to become No. 1.

No. 1 he became, within a season, and No. 1 he remained, until the rigours of 92 internationals—the most by any player in the history of the game—forced him to cry enough. By then he'd established himself as the master, awesomely strong in the scrum, a deadly accurate thrower to lineouts, a fearless leader by example and an inspirational captain. Laurie Mains said that he possessed that 'almost indefinable X-factor of which great All Black captains are made.'

The rapid decline in fortunes of Auckland (for whom he made 153 appearances), the Auckland Blues and the All Blacks following his retirement explains more vividly than any words the immense impact he made.

Sean Fitzpatrick scored his share of tries out on the wing. On occasions such as this he obviously thought he was one!

STATISTICS

	Period	Games	Tries	Points
Tests	86-97	92	12	55
NZ	86-97	128	20	90
Total	84-97	347	56	248

SID GOING

*Halfbacks didn't come any more elusive
or talented than Super Sid*

Michael Jones's refusal to play sport on Sundays because of his religious convictions has been widely publicised and cost the great Auckland loose forward countless test and representative appearances as well as participation in the third Rugby World Cup in South Africa.

But Jones wasn't the first All Black to take a stand on Sunday sport. Sid Going, whose All Black career extended across 11 seasons, was so committed to the Mormon faith he would neither train nor play on the Sabbath. 'I put rugby first on Tuesday and Thursday evenings and Saturday afternoons,' he says, 'and church first on Wednesday nights and Sundays.'

Because he operated in the amateur era before Sunday matches became common, Super Sid's commitment to his religion hardly impacted on his rugby career at all. He would sit on the sideline, along with his talented brothers Ken and Brian, at Northland's regular Sunday morning training sessions and observe. Coach Ted Griffin, a legendary character in the north, was happy to compromise because he knew what the Going brothers, Sid in particular, meant to his team.

Although many argued that Going's great rival Chris Laidlaw was the superior player, Griffin wouldn't have a bar of it. 'Sid could do everything Laidlaw could—and so much more,' he said. 'He could throw prodigious passes, taunt other halfbacks and because of his immense strength and great ball skills repeatedly slip through the tightest defensive screens.'

You know you've got a match-winner when opponents dedicate entire sessions to plotting tactics to stop you. That's how it was with Sid Going. The 1971 British Lions spent hours devising 'Stop Sid' strategies after he'd dominated the second test in Christchurch. Unfortunately for the All Blacks, who weren't alert enough to revert to Plan B, the Lions' neutralising tactics were so effective they went on to win the series.

Going's emergence at international level was delayed while he served the Mormon Church for three years in Canada as a missionary and he was 23 before he made his All Black debut against the Wallabies at Athletic Park in 1967. For the next few seasons he and Laidlaw vied for the test halfback role and it wasn't until Laidlaw headed for Oxford University (as a Rhodes Scholar) following the 1970 tour of South Africa that Going became secure in the position.

The qualities of elusiveness and strength—one leading correspondent lauded his 'rapid, violent attacks'—led to him scoring 33 tries in his 89 appearances for the All Blacks while Sid, Ken and Brian conspired to produce countless tries for North Auckland, their specialty being the bewildering triple-scissors move.

Going's immense talent didn't stop with his halfback's duties. On the 1970 All Black tour of South Africa, when the specialist goal-kickers were languishing, he took over the test goal-kicking duties with modest success. Probably his most famous goal was a sensational effort from three metres inside his own half to help North Auckland take the Ranfurly Shield from Auckland in 1971.

Since his retirement more than 20 years ago, Going has put an enormous amount back into rugby as a coach, most notably with Northland and as assistant coach of the Waikato Chiefs Super 12 team.

Of Sid Going's 86 appearances for the All Blacks none was more stunning than the Eden Park test against the French in 1968, when he scored two sensational solo tries.

*Super Sid was a
great stalwart of
the Northland team,
helping it win the
Ranfurly Shield
and making it
competitive against
overseas teams.*

75th
JUBILEE
NEW ZEALAND
RUGBY
FOOTBALL
UNION

New Zealand
v Australia
Athletic Park
August 19 1967

SOUVENIR PROGRAMME 20c

*Going's All Black debut
was in the 75th jubilee test
against Australia in 1967.*

72

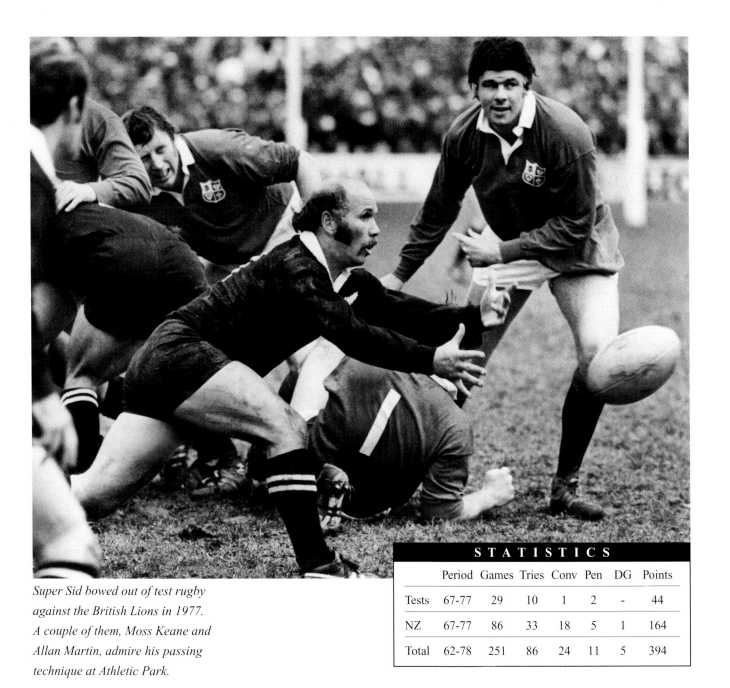

Super Sid bowed out of test rugby
against the British Lions in 1977.
A couple of them, Moss Keane and
Allan Martin, admire his passing
technique at Athletic Park.

STATISTICS

	Period	Games	Tries	Conv	Pen	DG	Points
Tests	67-77	29	10	1	2	-	44
NZ	67-77	86	33	18	5	1	164
Total	62-78	251	86	24	11	5	394

BRIAN LOCHORE

The quiet farmer who has become one of New Zealand sport's great statesmen

Brian Lochore justly deserves the title of statesman of New Zealand rugby. Yet he retains only one regret about his celebrated playing career which stretched over 13 seasons—that he allowed himself to be lured out of retirement in 1971 to make one last appearance for the All Blacks. He'd cried enough after returning as captain from the 1970 tour of South Africa, assuring his wife Pam that there would be no comebacks. 'A lot retire and then come back—not me, I'm finished,' he remembers saying.

That statement would come back to haunt him. First, Ivan Vodanovich telephoned midway through the 1971 series against the British Lions. It was crisis time for the All Black coach. Peter Whiting was out of the Wellington test with injury, Colin Meads was a doubtful starter and Ian Kirkpatrick was receiving injections for bruised ribs. Lochore was needed. Lochore resisted. Came a second call, this time from selector Bob Duff. *Your country needs you!*

'My reason for finally agreeing to play—having come back to help Wairarapa which also had key players injured—was because I felt I would be branded a so-and-so for not helping my country out.'

Lochore fronted up to lock the scrum with Meads. This was challenge enough since he'd played all his international rugby at No. 8. As it was, he gave an undistinguished performance and New Zealand lost 13–3, whereupon Lochore declared, very firmly, that he was going back into retirement.

But retirement as a player didn't mean retirement from rugby, which turned out to be a blessing for the game in New Zealand. The genial giant, who still farms at Hastwell near Masterton, would continue to make a massive contribution.

As a coach, he first hoisted Wairarapa-Bush from obscurity to first division NPC status, then claimed the World Cup after taking over the All Blacks. More importantly, he and another former All Black, Jock Hobbs, helped the NZRFU repel the WRC threat in 1995 by travelling throughout the country and convincing leading players they should contract themselves to the NZRFU.

Lochore broke into the big time as a player on the 1963–64 tour of the UK when Wilson Whineray was the captain. He was a bolter, particularly as the selectors named him as the No. 8—a position with which he was completely unfamiliar. 'It was strange I'd never played there,' he says, 'because it was obviously my position. Until then, I regarded myself as a flanker.'

He thrived in the No. 8 jersey and, with Waka Nathan nursing a broken jaw, won selection for the England and Scotland tests. It wasn't until 1965, however, that he cemented his place in the test pack. A year later there was astonishment when, following the retirement of Whineray, new coach Fred Allen named him as captain ahead of Meads and Kel Tremain. Allen had identified the special leadership qualities that Lochore possessed. 'He wasn't loud mouthed,' says Allen. 'He won control through his leadership and dynamic play.'

Lochore would remain undefeated as captain for four years, including a spectacular sweep through the UK in 1967. It was only in South Africa that he had to make a losing speech. There, his team dropped the series 3–1 despite producing sensational rugby throughout the provincial matches.

In 1999 he was knighted for his services to sport.

Brian Lochore, in his first season as captain in 1966, has things under control against the Lions at Christchurch. Poking between teammates Kel Tremain and Waka Nathan is Noel Murphy.

STATISTICS			
	Period	Games	Tries	Points
Tests	63-71	25	2	6
NZ	63-71	68	7	21
Total	59-71	202	20	60

THE GAMES

WHAT CONSTITUTES the ideal rugby game—one where there's a profusion of memorable tries scored by quality players, a close-fought encounter with a nail-biting finish, a contest of high drama where a team completes an astonishing comeback or simply an occasion when history is created through controversy or a sensational happening?

New Zealand rugby at both international and provincial level has been studded down the years with many famous examples such as these.

All Black folklore continues to thrive on the try Bob Deans was disallowed at Cardiff 95 years ago, on Cyril Brownlie's ordering off at Twickenham in 1925, on the Flood test at Eden Park in 1975 and the Flour Bomb test at the same location six years later.

While the All Blacks were involved in countless thrilling episodes throughout the century, for sheer excitement and drama (allied to parochial fervour) the greatest catalyst of all has surely been the Ranfurly Shield.

Almost 100 years of Shield challenges have produced many classic examples of pulsating finishes, heart-breaking losses and dramatic rescue acts. Two of rugby's greatest comeback victories are recorded in this chapter, both involving Auckland—Waka Nathan's last-gasp try to deny Canterbury victory in 1960, and the three-try explosion in the final eight minutes in 1996 that prevented Bay of Plenty taking possession of the famous trophy for the first time.

Three other Shield games feature—Otago's famous comeback win (this time at Auckland's expense) in 1947, Marlborough's David versus Goliath performance against Canterbury in 1973 and the epic Auckland-Canterbury game of 1985, which ranks as the Provincial Game of the Century.

Two games that qualify for inclusion fall into the 'unbelievable' category—Waikato's defeat of Danie Craven's Springboks in 1956 and the New Zealand Juniors' win over the All Blacks in 1973.

Contrasting with these are two modern but already legendary World Cup contests—New Zealand's sublime performance against England in 1995 and France's devastation of the All Blacks at Cardiff in 1999.

Memorable games come in many forms, all of which have been captured in this chapter.

'BEHIND THE POSTS, WAKA'

28 September 1960—Eden Park, Auckland—Ranfurly Shield
Auckland 19   Canterbury 18

It's not often a player in a challenging Ranfurly Shield team will kick five penalty goals and score a try and end up as a loser. But that's what happened with Canterbury midfield back Buddy Henderson, whose accurate boot up until the final minutes of the last Ranfurly Shield match of the 1960 season appeared to have him on the brink of hero status.

Canterbury had played well, and was leading holder Auckland 18–14 in a tight contest where it had gained the decisive edge in gradually wearing down the Auckland pack.

But that mid-week match, played before a large crowd of more than 30,000, is remembered not for Henderson's exploits but for the Shield-saving try of a young Auckland loose forward, Waka Nathan.

Just 20 and in his first full season with the Auckland A side, Nathan charged through to seize the ball as it bounced erratically away from the desperate Canterbury defence following a Mac Herewini kick.

'Behind the posts, Waka,' screamed All Black captain Wilson Whineray. Nathan followed the instruction by scoring under the crossbar, and the conversion by fullback Mike Cormack made the score 19–18.

Nathan's try was made possible when Auckland hooker Colin Currie stole a tighthead from All Black Dennis Young in the final scrum of the game—a huge relief for Nathan who admitted to 'feeling terrible' for earlier conceding a penalty that had allowed Canterbury to go ahead 15–14.

This rousing climax to the 1960 season was always going to be a thriller. Both sides had been strengthened by their All Blacks who had just returned from the tour of South Africa. Yet even without them, they had proven themselves the outstanding sides of the domestic season.

Auckland had endured a hiccup when North Auckland whisked the Shield away only to yield it in the return game 11 days later but had been convincing in repelling all of the subsequent late season challenges. Canterbury had also posted a string of big wins.

The game itself was long remembered for its many lead changes and as the last few minutes approached so certain were Auckland officials of their team's loss that they began to make appropriate arrangements for the presentation to Canterbury.

Even before the match there was drama. So bad were the traffic jams that the Auckland team arrived at Eden Park late, the kick-off being delayed 10 minutes, much to the annoyance of Canterbury officials who argued there were grounds for claiming the match by default.

During the match there was one incident which, if grim at the time, was later recalled with amusement. The great forward Kel Tremain, who was then with Auckland but the year before had been a Canterbury player, made a crack about the age of his marker in the lineout, Tiny Hill, referring to him as 'Grandpa'. Soon after, Tremain left the match, carried on a stretcher, and was one of the few Aucklanders oblivious to Nathan's last-minute heroics. Auckland coach Fred Allen also missed the match-saver because he was attending to Tremain.

The 1960 Auckland squad that retained the Ranfurly Shield—just!

Back row: *Jack Ross, Nev Bowerman, Paul Little, John Carter, Trevor Wynyard, Lew Fell, Harvey Leaf, Norm Brown.*

Third row: *Colin Currie, Tony Davies, Mike Cormack, John Barry, Wilson Whineray, Geoff Perry, Barry Thomas, Warren Moran, Frank McMullen.*

Second row: *Don Dormer, 'Snow' White, Pat Simperingham, Bernie Bowerman, Kel Tremain, Murray Reid, Peter Priestly, Frank Colthurst.*

Front row: *Waka Nathan, Fred Allen (coach), Bob Graham (captain), Merv Corner (president), Des Connor (vice-captain), Johnny Simpson (assistant coach), Don McKay.*

In front: *Tony Edgar, Bob McMullen, Steve Nesbit, John Brady, Mac Herewini, John Sibun.*

CANTERBURY
v
AUCKLAND
for the
RANFURLY SHIELD
at
EDEN PARK
Auckland
Wednesday, September 28,
1960

AUCKLAND RUGBY UNION OFFICIAL PUBLICATION   Price 1/.

ENGLAND OVERWHELMED

18 June 1995—Newlands, Cape Town—World Cup semi-final
New Zealand 45   England 29

All Black teams always prepare diligently for major challenges although there probably has never been a better-prepared New Zealand team than Laurie Mains' World Cup side of 1995 as it approached the semi-final against England at Cape Town.

The planning for that encounter had started four months earlier at a training camp in Taupo when Mains and Co. had devised tactics appropriate to each opponent. The All Blacks didn't know they would be playing England when they left New Zealand because they were on opposite sides of the draw but they weren't taking any chances.

'I had this feeling,' confessed Mains later, 'one I couldn't easily explain that New Zealand and England were fated to meet during the tournament. I think it was because I wanted to play them, to avenge the defeat we'd suffered at Twickenham in 1993, and because the arrogance their players and management exhibited following their win rankled with us.'

Mains knew England to be a clinical side. 'So we went out to deliberately play unconventional rugby against them. As far back as February we had plotted tactics specifically designed to neutralise them.'

Little did Mains suspect that the innovative tactics he would release against England would not only sweep the pride of Northern Hemisphere rugby away but would revolutionise the game worldwide. They would also be instrumental in Rupert Murdoch's decision to invest a cool $US500 million in Southern Hemisphere rugby.

So meticulous was the preparation that, after winning the toss, captain Sean Fitzpatrick and manager Colin Meads approached the referee (Irishman Steve Hilditch) and warned him that the kick-off would be unorthodox. They didn't want him getting in the way!

The surprise kick-off—away from the forwards—worked like a dream. England captain Will Carling knocked on, conceding the scrum from which the All Blacks set up Jonah Lomu for the first of his four sensational tries.

Lomu would seize the headlines from this remarkable encounter—deservedly so because he was truly awesome. He was fuelled by his opponent Tony Underwood who in an interview with a South African newspaper after the quarter-finals had asked, 'Who's Jonah? He hasn't marked anyone yet.' Underwood compounded that mistake by winking at Jonah prior to kick-off.

Lomu was unstoppable, running around, away from and, as happened to fullback Mike Catt, over the top of bewildered Englishmen to score a remarkable four tries. His first try—which has been replayed hundreds of times since—provided the All Blacks with the perfect start, barely two minutes after kick-off.

Not two minutes later, they were in again after capitalising on the instinctive genius of Walter Little, who outrageously elected to attack from inside his 22 from the restart. 'I could see they were shell-shocked from Jonah's try,' he said, 'and unprepared for another onslaught, so we let 'em have one.' This time Josh Kronfeld scored and after four minutes New Zealand was ahead 12–0.

As the English fans sat dazed, the All Blacks maintained their incredible momentum. A stunning 40-metre dropped goal from Zinzan Brooke added to the try feast and before the English knew it, they were 35–3 behind. A late rally that produced four tries salvaged a little pride for England but it was far too little too late.

While Mains and his players had been confident that they could unsettle England from the start, they had never dreamed their well-plotted tactics would reap such rewards. It was game, set and match, and the All Blacks were bound for the World Cup final at Ellis Park, with England condemned to the play-off at Loftus Versfeld.

It was the try that announced to the world that Jonah Lomu had arrived—here he steamrollers Mike Catt on the way to the first of his four touchdowns against England in the 1995 Rugby World Cup.

'NO DOUBT ABOUT IT—IT WAS A TRY'

16 December 1905—Arms Park, Cardiff
Wales 3 New Zealand 0

No other All Black test has had as much ink devoted to it as that against Wales at Cardiff Arms Park on 16 December 1905. All those who watched it or participated in it have long since passed away. But the controversy that surrounded that match still lingers. Wales, which had an extremely strong side then, won this first ever clash between the two nations, 3–0. But there has always been dispute as to whether the game should have been at least a draw or a 5–3 All Blacks win.

Of course, the narrow Welsh win remains the one and only blot on the remarkable record achieved by the 1905–06 Originals who defeated England, Ireland and Scotland decisively while most of their other opponents were thrashed by startling margins.

Ever since, certainly from within New Zealand, there have been claims that the Scottish referee John Dallas, who was wearing street clothes and frequently had difficulty keeping up with play, erred in not allowing a try to All Black Bob Deans.

The legendary incident occurred in the second spell with Wales leading 3-0 following a try by winger Teddy Morgan. The great Billy Wallace, playing on the wing for the All Blacks, instigated a break and threw a long, clear pass to Deans who, as he approached the line, was tackled by Morgan.

Deans, even on his deathbed just four years later—he died tragically young—insisted he had made the goal-line. His claims were always supported throughout his life by Wallace. As recently as 1969, Wallace (who lived to the grand old age of 94) said in an interview: 'There's no doubt about it—it was a try.'

The Welsh player who was the closest witness, Morgan, admitted in subsequent years Deans had gone over the line. The try, had it been awarded, was a comfortable distance from the goalposts and a conversion from the accurate boot of Wallace was highly likely.

But then, as now, the referee's word was all that mattered.

In many ways it was beneficial to posterity that the try wasn't allowed. The incident only enhanced the game's folklore, creating the solitary loss on an historic tour. It in no way diminished the legend of the 1905 All Blacks, instead helping foster an intense rugby rivalry between New Zealand and Wales that has flourished to this day.

There's also reason to believe that, on the run of play, Wales may have deserved to win in what was a generally even contest. In his 1969 interview, Wallace recalled that Wales in 1905 was 'a great side and we struck them at a bad time—near the end of the tour with only 13 fit men'.

New Zealand and Wales battling it out in 1905. The All Blacks wore long shorts while the Welsh players wore a mixture of knickerbockers and longs. Notice the referee wearing a suit!

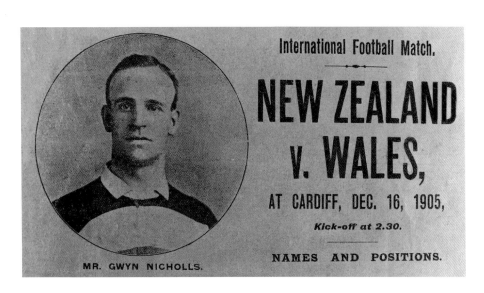

International Football Match.

NEW ZEALAND
v. WALES,

AT CARDIFF, DEC. 16, 1905,

Kick-off at 2.30.

NAMES AND POSITIONS.

MR. GWYN NICHOLLS.

MIGHTY MOOLOOS CAPTURE BOK HEAD

9 June 1956—Rugby Park, Hamilton
Waikato 14   South Africa 10

A generation of New Zealanders will never forget the 1956 Springboks' tour of this country. Seldom before and certainly never since has rugby etched itself into the national fibres in a way that goes beyond sport.

What made this tour special was that it became a series where the New Zealand desire to win became something of a crusade. It was a quest to remove what had become New Zealand rugby's biggest bogey. Although rugby was well-established as the national sport, one goal had proven elusive. In series against the Springboks in 1921, 1928, 1937 and 1949, the All Blacks had had two draws and two decisive defeats, including in 1949 a 4–0 whitewash.

So in every Kiwi heart revenge for the humiliations of 1937 and 1949 became a priority. The pattern from what was one of the most passionate seasons in New Zealand rugby history was set with the tour's opening game and a match now celebrated in folklore.

Waikato was given the first match against the Springboks and it must have quickly become apparent to the tourists that its management, led by Danie Craven, might have been better advised to have insisted on a more gentle introduction.

Waikato boasted such famous players as the Clarke brothers, Don and Ian, hooker Ron Hemi and halfback Ponty Reid, who would go on to become a test captain. A few seasons before it had enjoyed a notable run with the Ranfurly Shield, during which the Mooloo mascot became its symbol. It was still among the country's best provincial teams.

Under the shrewd coaching of Dick Everest, it had the strategy and the motivation to take the game to the Springboks in inspired fashion.

In the opening minutes came a try by winger Malcolm McDonald that was followed in rapid order by a Don Clarke dropped goal and a conversion of a try scored by Rex Pickering, a flanker who because of an injury had been posted to the wing (in the days before replacements were permitted). A further penalty goal by Clarke had Waikato ahead 14–0 by half-time, to the rapturous delight of the 31,000 who had crammed into Rugby Park, which had an official capacity of 28,000.

Although the Springboks rallied for two second-spell converted tries, Waikato hung on gamely for a 14–10 win. It was a heroic effort—not least because an injury to midfield back Jack Bullick meant Waikato played much of the game with only 14 men.

And so in the first outing of their three-month tour of New Zealand, the South Africans had to hand across the Springbok head, traditionally awarded to the first province to beat them. It was a psychological blow from which they never completely recovered and they eventually lost the test series 3–1.

Twenty-two matches later, a forlorn Craven uttered a sentence which sent the country into delirium: 'It's all yours, New Zealand.'

Jan Pickard was described in the Springbok pen portraits in 1956 as 'a bullocking player with amazing strength'. That's him pulling down lineout possession in the tour opener, sensationally lost to Waikato.

Mooloo bears the autographs of the 1956 Waikato players who assured themselves of everlasting fame by defeating the Springboks.

85

RED DEVILS HAVE THE LAST LAUGH

28 July 1973—Lancaster Park, Christchurch—Ranfurly Shield
Marlborough 13   Canterbury 6

New Zealand provincial rugby has known arguably no bigger upset than Marlborough's 13–6 Ranfurly Shield win over Canterbury in 1973, a victory by one of the country's smallest unions over one of the largest and most consistently successful.

The gap between provincial unions wasn't as large then as it later became. It was still possible in the 1970s to become an All Black playing for smaller unions, as indeed was so with two of the Marlborough players—No. 8 Alan Sutherland and winger Brian Ford.

Marlborough's cause was also helped by having its challenge grossly underrated if not by the players certainly by the Canterbury officials.

The true worth of the Canterbury team was revealed later in the year when it won 11 matches on the trot, including a defeat of England. But for that Shield game, the first of the year and in July, Canterbury went into the game underdone and with minimal preparation.

It faced a side that contained Brian Ford, Alan and brother Ray Sutherland, as well as such footballers as Jim Joseph (father of All Black Jamie), David Neal and Tony Goddard. Against such players, Canterbury's complacency was to prove fatal.

Marlborough—or the Red Devils as they were sometimes dubbed in the media—besides being a competent side well led by Ray Sutherland and coached by former All Black winger Ralph Caulton, possessed a secret weapon. It was remembered that during World War II as a serviceman the great coach Fred Allen had played a game for Marlborough. So Allen was persuaded to come to Blenheim to give the team a pep talk. He then gave a second talk that was put on tape and played to the players just before kick-off. In the words of Alan Sutherland, the Allen oratory made the Marlborough players feel '10 feet tall and invincible'.

The game itself was played before a moderate attendance, many of whom were from Marlborough. Canterbury dominated the first spell but could score only once, a try to Duncan Hales which Fergie McCormick converted. With Marlborough's Graeme Cocks kicking two penalty goals, it was 6–6 at half-time.

It stayed that way for much of the second spell before Goddard broke the deadlock with a dropped goal. And then four minutes from time Ford broke into the clear and with a superb run beat even the renowned defence of McCormick for the decisive try.

Marlborough would repulse six challenges for the Shield before losing it in 1974 to South Canterbury. Yet for Marlborough, Ford remains a hero forever. Even then, for such a small union to topple one of the country's largest was the stuff of legends.

Victories by minnows in Ranfurly Shield challenge matches are rare, but Marlborough managed it in 1973, defeating Canterbury at Lancaster Park. A delighted Tony Goddard shows what winning the trophy meant to the Red Devils.

FURIOUS VIC SORTS OUT HIS SOUTHERNERS

20 August 1947—Carisbrook, Dunedin—Ranfurly Shield
Otago 18   Auckland 12

They didn't call it the House of Pain 50 years ago, but Carisbrook in Dunedin represented just as daunting a challenge for visiting teams then as it does now.

The Ranfurly Shield—an elusive treasure down Otago way over the last four decades—was almost impossible to prise away from the men in dark blue in the late 1940s.

Otago was then superbly drilled by Vic Cavanagh Jnr, a legendary character among New Zealand rugby coaches, and successfully defended the Shield on 20 consecutive occasions until finally yielding it to Canterbury in 1950.

There were some magnificent performances by Cavanagh's team, including a 31–0 whipping of Canterbury. Tries counted only three points in those days, so the result is equivalent to what would now be 45–0.

The contest in those halcyon days of the Deep South which has come to epitomise the Otago Shield era of the 1940s was a 1947 match against a strong Auckland side boasting such famous players as Bob Scott, Fred Allen, Johnny Simpson and Percy Tetzlaff.

Yet at half-time, with the score at 12–3 to Auckland, the match appeared lost. With tries then worth three points and the laws allowing the ball to be kicked out from anywhere on the field, a lead of nine points was regarded as almost insurmountable.

So the 26,000 who were crammed into Carisbrook for this midweek challenge had by the interval resigned themselves to seeing the Shield move north. Their pessimism was heightened by the comprehensive manner with which Otago had been outplayed in the first half. To two tries by centre Les Deas, a conversion by Scott and a dropped goal by the first-five Bandy Ewert, Otago replied with a solitary penalty goal by Laurie Haig.

But in the second half the match was transformed. And if the legend that still persists in Otago is true, the man primarily responsible was coach Cavanagh—regarded as one of rugby's most influential figures and deepest thinkers.

There are two popular versions as to what happened. One is that he gave the team the silent treatment as they glumly went out for the second half, farewelling them with an insulting, 'Out you go, girls.' The other is that he poured on the players five minutes of non-stop hysterical abuse.

Neither of these is apparently correct. The most convincing recollection is that, true to his logical nature, he calmly pin-pointed areas where mistakes had been made and their remedies. These Otago put to such effect that with tries to John Tanner and Ron Elvidge, a Haig conversion and penalty goal and a Jimmy Kearney dropped goal (then worth four points), it recovered to win 18–12.

Two years later many of these Otago and Auckland players were in the All Black side which toured South Africa. But Cavanagh wasn't sent with them as coach, an omission by the NZRFU that has remained puzzling ever since.

Auckland first-five 'Bandy' Ewert prises the ball away from the toe of Otago loose forward Doug Hamilton during the epic 1947 challenge match at Carisbrook.

TIDE'S IN

14 June 1975— Eden Park, Auckland
New Zealand 24   Scotland 0

Aucklanders are accustomed to wet winters. Indeed, it's not unusual for rain to fall there virtually every day for more than two months during June and July. And in summer, torrential downpours are common.

But it's unusual for two months' rain to tumble from the clouds in 24 hours, which is what happened in the Queen City in mid-June 1975. Unfortunately, the deluge coincided with the Scottish international at Eden Park, the climax to their seven-match tour.

The rain settled in on the Friday afternoon (Friday the 13th, would you believe!) and was unrelenting until late Saturday. Thirteen centimetres fell, causing flooding throughout the city and leaving the emergency services at full stretch.

At any venue other than Eden Park, the test would unquestionably have been abandoned. But because of its volcanic base, Eden Park has always been a good draining ground, though this was the ultimate test.

When the officials of the two teams inspected the ground approximately an hour before the scheduled kick-off, they were surprised at how firm the surface was. The ground itself was definitely playable—the concern was the lakes that had formed around the perimeter as effectively as moats.

Scotland manager George Burrell agreed to the game going ahead. It was impracticable to postpone the event because Scotland was flying out to the UK the next day.

The fire brigade arrived and began pumping water away in the hour before the start, although it didn't seem to make a great deal of difference. Astonishingly—considering that the rain was still pelting down—some 40,000 people were present when the game started. Many had planned to wear sporty gear but turned out in parkas, shorts, bare feet and every range of wet-weather gear ever invented.

While the Scots were experienced at playing in cold conditions, they'd never experienced anything like this. Funnily enough, the All Blacks had in Sydney just 12 months earlier. On that occasion it wasn't just rain but a biting 80 kph southerly as well, laced with hail and almost sub-zero temperatures.

So the All Blacks knew how to play in the wet. It was all pretty logical, really. Where there is a lot of rain or mud, there are obviously going to be a lot of lineouts. It is important, therefore, to make the lineouts a strength, not a weakness. On Eden Park, they became a strength for the All Blacks, a weakness for Scotland.

The New Zealanders didn't tap the ball back to Sid Going and wish him luck as the Scots poured through onto him. They deployed one forward—usually Ian Kirkpatrick who had filled the role so magnificently in Sydney—to take the tapdowns from John Callesen and Hamish Macdonald. Then Kirkpatrick would deliver the ball to Going when he felt everything was under control.

There were some 75 lineouts, of which only 46 were decisive. New Zealand won 28, nearly all cleanly. Scotland won 18, most of them producing 'bad ball' for halfback Douglas Morgan.

In conditions where a nil–all scoreline might have been expected, the All Blacks scored four outstanding tries, two of them by dynamic winger Bryan Williams and the others by Hamish Macdonald and Duncan Robertson. Joe Karam made light of the sodden ball to land all four conversions.

The All Blacks had prevailed in the conditions, handling the ball impeccably, while the Scots had blundered their way through 80 minutes. Scottish captain Ian McLauchlan cried in the dressing room, in sheer disappointment. 'What can you do,' he asked, 'when your backs can't catch the ball?'

The tide's in! Why the 1975 Scottish international at Eden Park became known as the Flood Test is graphically obvious from this photo.

ERRATIC GENIUSES DOWN THE ALL BLACKS

31 October 1999—Twickenham, London—World Cup semi-final
France 43   New Zealand 31

John Hart isn't the first All Black coach to curse the unpredictability of the French. Eric Watson in 1979 and Laurie Mains on three occasions in the mid-nineties were others who rued that Gallic flair.

But their disappointments pale into insignificance alongside the second-half events during the second of the 1999 Rugby World Cup semi-finals at Twickenham.

The first semi-final had been sensational enough with the golden boot of Jannie de Beer placing a difficult, wide-angle penalty goal in injury time to take play into extra time. The deadlock was eventually broken by an astonishing 48-metre dropped goal from Wallaby flyhalf Stephen Larkham.

And so to that traumatic second semi-final. Although the French had exposed frailties in the All Black backline in the action-packed first half, there appeared an inevitability about the outcome. Hart's men were universally expected to win by 30 or 40 points. Especially when the crowd's favourite, Jonah Lomu, combined gloriously with Jeff Wilson to secure a second try and give his team a commanding 24–10 advantage.

Former captain (and now NZRFU president) Andy Dalton always used to say you couldn't relax against the French until you were more than two converted tries in front. You needed that margin because of what he described as their 'erratic genius'.

A pity he wasn't on the field at Twickenham on 31 October to alert the men in black, because the 'erratic geniuses' seized control and in 26 minutes transformed a straightforward contest into a colossal upset.

The French onslaught started gently enough with a pair of dropped goals by Christophe Lamaison. He had come on at flyhalf when Thomas Castaignede cried off injured and Lamaison had much to do with the team's World Cup revival, particularly after he added two penalty goals.

That made it 22–24. Now we had a contest. The crowd, earlier content to sit back and essentially be entertained by superstars like Lomu, perked up and took a closer interest.

After the second of Lamaison's droppies, Abdelatif Benazzi, the veteran French lock, inspired his colleagues by assuring them he saw panic in the eyes of the All Blacks. 'Now we have them,' he said.

They 'had them' indeed. Winger Christophe Dominici, who challenged dynamic flanker Olivier Magne for player of the day honours and who had created France's first-half try with a sensational scything run, put his team in front with a stunning kick-and-retrieve try.

The next five-pointer went to Richard Dourthe from a pin-point kick through by Lamaison, after the French had almost arrogantly taken a lineout instead of a kick at goal. The *coup de grâce* was provided by winger Philippe Bernat-Salles who won a thrilling 75-metre chase after a rare, and desperate, All Black attack had broken down.

The French had scored 33 points in 26 minutes and blown the World Cup favourites (red-hot favourites at that) clean off the park. The final scoreline of 43–31 represented a 59-point turnaround. At their previous meeting, at Athletic Park in June, France had suffered an embarrassing 54–7 defeat. Lomu apart—and the big man scored two classic tries—the All Blacks were outplayed in all departments.

Although they would be shut down by the Wallabies in the final a week later, the French were given a massive boost by this victory, which brought the World Cup dramatically to life.

Frenchmen Franck Tournaire (3) and Olivier Brouzet (20) celebrate another try at the All Blacks' expense during the dramatic World Cup semi-final.

THE PROVINCIAL MATCH OF THE CENTURY

14 September 1985—Lancaster Park, Christchurch—Ranfurly Shield
Auckland 28   Canterbury 23

There has never been a Ranfurly Shield reign as momentous as Auckland's sequence of repelling 61 challenges from 1985 to 1993, a record which almost trebled the previous best and one that almost certainly will never be beaten.

So it's appropriate that such a magnificent chapter in New Zealand provincial rugby history began on an auspicious note. To start the era, Auckland had to take the Shield from a Canterbury side, which under the coaching of Alex Wyllie had proven itself a champion unit.

At Lancaster Park, in front of a crowd that spilled well beyond the ground's capacity of about 50,000, Auckland beat Canterbury 28–23. And if this was not the greatest Shield match of all time, then it certainly has to be rated in the top handful of challenge matches.

It was a game which underwent an unprecedented media buildup with a huge national debate being generated because of the then strict NZRFU policy that did not allow for live telecasts.

That the game was likely to be a great showdown could be discerned by the excellent records each team had compiled during the mid-eighties.

Under Wyllie, Canterbury had defended the Shield 25 times to equal the record sequence set by Auckland between 1960 and 1963. Auckland, coached by John Hart and spilling over with such cel-ebrated All Blacks as Andy Haden, Gary and Alan Whetton, Grant Fox, Joe Stanley and John Kirwan, had been just as impressive in sweeping to the 1984 NPC first division title.

Such was the hype preceding the match that there was a danger of it becoming an anticlimax. But even allowing for some defensive deficiencies, it was a thriller and many have proclaimed it 'the provincial match of the century'.

In the first half, as Auckland raced to a 24–0 half-time lead, it did seem as if some of the worst fears would be realised. Tries by Stanley, Kirwan, Terry Wright and John Drake were scored with such ease that it seemed what had been a fine Canterbury reign would end ingloriously in a rout.

But apart from an early Steve McDowell try, the second spell was as much Canterbury's as the first had been Auckland's. Bruce Deans, Craig Green, Wayne Smith and Albert Anderson scored tries and in the final minute a Smith up-and-under nearly brought a fifth. Instead, the madly bouncing ball was tapped dead by a now desperate Auckland hand.

So a great Shield era ended as another, to be even greater, was about to begin. But as with the 1974 Joe Frazier–Muhammad Ali 'thriller in Manila' heavyweight boxing bout and the 1980 Bjorn Borg–John McEnroe Wimbledon tennis final, this was one of those rare contests where there was no real loser.

They would be All Blacks together in the late eighties but in 1985 when Auckland lifted the
Ranfurly Shield from Canterbury, Joe Stanley and Bruce Deans were key individuals in their provincial teams.

'DON'T WORRY, SKIP'

13 August 1960—Free State Stadium, Bloemfontein
South Africa 11 New Zealand 11

Desperate situations demand desperate measures, and at the highest level of sport that is when champions come to the fore.

The 1960 All Blacks who toured South Africa were fortunate to possess their share of champions—none greater than captain Wilson Whineray and the giant goal-kicking fullback Don Clarke.

Together, they contrived to salvage a test match (and a series) that to all intents and purposes was dead and buried. In that era of three-point tries, an eight-point deficit with scarcely five minutes remaining represented a crisis of extreme magnitude.

And that's how things were at the Free State Stadium in Bloemfontein with time running out in the third test of a desperately tight series. The Springboks had claimed the first test in Pretoria, the All Blacks levelling things up in Cape Town. So for the sake of the series, a victory was imperative at Bloemfontein.

The New Zealanders were down 3–11 with 75 minutes played—a situation about as bad as it could be. But there came a flicker of hope when the great Springbok flanker Martin Pelser (whose achievements on the rugby field were the more remarkable because he was blind in one eye) put himself offside 55 metres from his goalposts.

Clarke, who could kick the ball massive distances at sea level, certainly relished the high altitude, which added metres to his goal-kicking range, as he demonstrated by placing the goal to narrow the margin to five points.

Whineray, an inspirational captain, told his players to abandon caution, to go for broke. As Colin Meads later wrote in his biography, 'The remote possibility of the draw was worth 10 times the chance of a slightly greater defeat.'

It was Kel Tremain who in the dying moments set the All Blacks rolling forward, committing the Springbok centre Ian Kirkpatrick to the tackle. When New Zealand then claimed the ruck, it meant the South Africans were a player short in defence.

In his haste, halfback Kevin Briscoe threw a shocker of a pass, which missed first-five Steve Nesbit altogether and bobbled along to Terry Lineen in midfield. Briscoe's lapse momentarily threw the defence off guard and there was hesitancy as Kevin Laidlaw received the ball and bolted half through a gap. As Springbok fullback Lionel Wilson came at him, Laidlaw placed a pin-point grubber kick through for winger Frank McMullen to run on to.

The result was a sensationally well-taken try in the corner, which left the crowd stunned. The responsibility now fell upon the broad shoulders of Don Clarke to land the conversion which would salvage a draw and keep the series alive till the final test at Port Elizabeth.

A lesser mortal might have found the experience overwhelming. He was being asked to take a decisive wide-angle conversion in the dying moments of the match in front of a wildly partisan crowd. But Clarke was sublimely confident. 'Don't worry, skip,' he told Whineray as he took the ball from him.

Don's brother Ian was running touch (as happened in those days) and almost before the ball had left his boot, he had his flag in the air.

Many of his teammates weren't so sure. Some couldn't watch. But once the ball sailed between the uprights, there was incredible relief and celebrating. Thanks to The Boot, the series was still alive.

Frank McMullen's last-minute try against the Springboks at Bloemfontein in 1960
kept alive his team's chances of salvaging the game and the series. It still needed the conversion.
'Don't worry, skip,' Don Clarke said to his captain and promptly slotted the wide-angle kick.

SOUTH AFRICA SUID-AFRIKA
VERSUS TEEN
NEW ZEALAND NIEU-SEELAND

THIRD TEST   DERDE TOETS
BLOEMFONTEIN   BLOEMFONTEIN
13th AUGUST, 1960   13 AUGUSTUS 1960

WATSON'S WONDERS UPSET THE MEN IN BLACK

1 August 1973—Carisbrook, Dunedin
NZ Juniors 14   New Zealand 10

The All Blacks have suffered their share of embarrassing defeats down the years but it's doubtful that any of them have caused greater mortification than the loss to the New Zealand Juniors in a mid-weeker at Carisbrook in 1973.

The Juniors, coached by Eric Watson and captained by Bruce Gemmell, outclassed their seniors 14–10, a result that sent the 18,000 spectators away shaking their heads.

It was an unusual set of circumstances that led to the All Blacks and the Juniors doing battle, because the Springboks were supposed to be touring in 1973. But when the Labour Government came to power, Prime Minister Norman Kirk called the tour off, leaving the NZRFU with an empty international calendar.

Scotland loomed as a likely replacement, but when it declined the NZRFU put together a four-match internal tour for the All Blacks (featuring two hits with the President's Invitation XV and games against the Juniors and the Maoris).

A match with the Juniors obviously seemed like a gentle way to ease the All Blacks into the new season, the previous one having ended traumatically with losses to France and the Barbarians at the end of a long, demanding European tour (the one from which Keith Murdoch had been sent home).

The All Blacks had a new mentor, J. J. Stewart, the third coach in 15 months (following on from Jack Gleeson and Bob Duff). Although he would produce excellent results at international level, he was on a no-win assignment in 1973.

Key players were missing, for various reasons, and the domestic tour had stirred little enthusiasm among the country's leading players. Most of them seemed to regard Dunedin as more of a reunion than a rugby challenge. They found it difficult to build killer instinct against their own juniors especially when the two teams had been transported from the airport to their hotels in the same bus.

Coach Stewart had 24 hours to try and whip his new-look team into shape against the match-hardened Juniors who had played eight matches around New Zealand leading into this game.

Without Andy Haden, who was being saved for the Saturday game, and Peter Whiting, who'd injured his knee in a club game the previous Saturday, the All Blacks were seriously under-equipped in the lineouts, being forced to use Graham Whiting, a specialist prop, as a lock and jumper. The result was that the Juniors' ace John Callesen had himself an absolute feast in the lineouts, securing the quality ball the All Blacks thirsted for.

The All Blacks led 7–3 at half-time and 10–7 inside the final quarter but a penalty goal by fullback Richard Wilson tied it all up and then a spectacular, diving try by winger Terry Mitchell completed the humiliation of the national team whose solitary try had been scored by Grant Batty.

If the nation thought that set-back would spur the All Blacks to greatness, they were wrong. Three days later, they lost to the President's XV 35–28 at Athletic Park. Coach Stewart, maintaining his humour in the face of adversity, announced that if his team lost three in a row, he would bare his buttocks outside the Auckland Town Hall. He was saved this embarrassment when the All Blacks came through to defeat New Zealand Maori 18–8, going on to win the rematch against the Invitation XV 22–10.

The day the juniors beat the masters. New Zealand Juniors captain Bruce Gemmell is chaired off Carisbrook by Jim Carroll and John Callesen after their stunning win.

CARRINGTON SAVES THE DAY

11 August 1996—Eden Park, Auckland—Ranfurly Shield
Auckland 30 Bay of Plenty 29

If Counties is supreme as the union with the greatest store of unlucky Ranfurly Shield experiences, Bay of Plenty merits a special mention for two unforgettable challenges—74 years apart—which fall into the category of Two That Got Away.

Bay of Plenty's initial agony story relates to the team's challenge against Hawkes Bay at Nelson Park in Hastings in 1922, three weeks after the Magpies had lifted the trophy from Wellington.

With time up, Bay of Plenty, which had had much the better of the game, scored a try beside the goalposts to make the score 16–17. The conversion appeared a formality and the Hawkes Bay officials began preparing to hand over the Shield.

But the conversion was causing consternation within the Bay of Plenty team. Skipper Lex McLean, who had shared the goal-kicking duties, called up his halfback, Boucher.

Hawkes Bay coach Norman McKenzie later recalled the drama: 'This little chap [Boucher] got an attack of the staggers at once. Trembling like a leaf, he placed the ball, with his teammates tendering plenty of advice. He retired to kick, went forward and replaced the ball, and finally let drive—and almost missed the ball altogether!'

It would be hard to imagine a more excruciating Shield experience than that but Bay of Plenty managed it at Eden Park in August 1996 when it came up against Graham Henry's Auckland team while the All Blacks were still touring South Africa.

Bay of Plenty was then coached by Gordon Tietjens, who would later attain greatness as a sevens coach. Even so, it was a side of modest talent, and had failed to progress beyond the semi-finals of the NPC second division the previous season. It was not expected to stay 80 minutes with the blues. Well, with 10 minutes remaining, Bay of Plenty had established a seemingly unassailable 29–11 advantage, by which stage Henry was preparing a losing speech.

But three tries in eight minutes, the final one by 19-year-old Matt Carrington with 33 seconds on the clock, allowed Auckland to complete one of the most incredible comeback chapters in Shield history.

When prop Kevin Nepia powered across to make it 29–16, Auckland captain Eroni Clarke felt a miracle was still possible. 'I realised two converted tries would do it,' he said. 'I felt we had just enough time, if we did everything right.'

The Bay of Plenty players, having given everything, were now like punch-drunk boxers, virtually out on their feet. They began to fall off tackles and allowed winger James Kerr to crash over in the corner. Carrington converted brilliantly from touch.

Time for one last attack, but when Auckland knocked on, the opportunity, surely, was lost. About 50 seconds remained when Bay halfback Joe Tauiwi fed to the fateful last scrum. The crowd (11,000 of them) were electrified when Auckland claimed a tighthead from the exhausted Bay front rowers.

The lifeline had been offered to Clarke's men, Clarke himself creating the match-saving score with a deft kick through which Carrington retrieved to score, albeit wide out.

Everything now hung on Carrington's wide-angle conversion. 'Take your time,' said Clarke. 'Don't miss, don't miss!' implored teammate Brian Lima. Carrington remained totally focused and sent the ball straight between the uprights.

How did that one get away? Shattered Bay of Plenty players try to comprehend
a scoreboard that had read 29–11 to them 10 minutes earlier.

THE FLOUR BOMB TEST

12 September 1981—Eden Park, Auckland
New Zealand 25   South Africa 22

So many diversions happened in the incredible 1981 third test between the All Blacks and the Springboks at Eden Park that the actual rugby tended to get shoved into the background.

This was the match where frustrations over the controversial tour and apartheid in sport exploded into crisis. A light plane continually buzzed the ground and dropped flour bombs, one of which hit All Black prop Gary Knight.

And there was violence around the streets of Eden Park as police battled to keep demonstrators under control. It was truly an occasion where the images of petrol drums and barbed wire prevailed and many New Zealanders, whether for the tour or against, felt a numb sickness.

If judged purely as a rugby event, as many would have preferred it to have been, it was a sensational game. Had it not been for the exceptional circumstances, controversy would probably have lingered for many years over the manner in which the All Blacks won the match 25–22.

As the game came to its final few minutes it was poised at 22–all and many were of the mind that that would not have been a bad note on which to have finished. It would have reflected the similar quality of each side and a tied series and a drawn match would have been in keeping with the tenor of the entire All Black-Springbok relationship. For there were many genuinely convinced at the time that politics had ended one of world sport's most intense rivalries.

As it happened, it was to be another 11 years before the two countries met again, officially anyway, on the rugby field. But referee Clive Norling became the dominant figure in the dramatic final few minutes—for two reasons both of which made New Zealanders thankful a Welshman and not one of their own had made the calls. The first was that play dragged on long after what should have been the scheduled final whistle. The other was the penalty award a minute from time which broke the deadlock.

Norling's cruel call was against the Springboks for not retiring 10 metres when replacement halfback Mark Donaldson tapped and ran from a free kick. Norling then gave a penalty and from about 36 metres Allan Hewson landed the goal.

It was a happy atonement for Hewson in particular. The All Blacks had taken a 16–3 half-time lead, with wing Stu Wilson and Knight scoring tries and the forwards—among whom a 21-year-old Gary Whetton was making his test debut—had gained the edge. And then the Springboks stormed back brilliantly. Winger Ray Mordt scored three tries at the expense of Hewson's defensive frailties. All this added to the pressure on Hewson as he took his match-saving kick. To his credit, it never looked like missing. But it must have seemed to the Springboks at that moment that the whole world was against them.

Another flour bomb raid from the Cessna as it comes in low over Eden Park during the final match of the controversial 1981 Springbok tour.

MAURICE BROWNLIE TAKES CHARGE

3 January 1925—Twickenham, London
New Zealand 17   England 11

As the first New Zealand team to go through a tour of Britain unbeaten, the 1924–25 All Blacks occupy one of the highest places in rugby folklore and are still known by their nickname, 'The Invincibles'.

Only the fact that Scotland, whose union was miffed over arrangements made for the 1905 tour, wasn't included on the itinerary prevented them achieving the Grand Slam, a feat the All Blacks had to wait until 1978 to accomplish.

In all, the Invincibles played 32 matches for 32 wins in England, Wales, Ireland, France and British Columbia, scoring 838 points while conceding only 116.

By the time of their international against England, which came near the tour's end and was the last in Britain, the 1924–25 All Blacks, described by critics before they left as one of the worst to leave these shores, had been remarkably successful.

But the true seal of greatness came with the win over England, which under the captaincy of Wavell Wakefield, later a prominent administrator and politician, fielded a powerful side.

What embellished the legend of the Invincibles was that the 17–11 win at Twickenham—which followed victories over Ireland by 6–0 and Wales by 19–0—was gained with only 14 men.

Early in the game after a couple of skirmishes between the packs and a warning from Welsh referee Albert Freethy, one of the All Black forwards, Cyril Brownlie, was ordered off for allegedly kicking another man. For another 43 years, Brownlie was the only international to suffer this indignity.

Brownlie's teammates were so enraged by what they saw as an injustice that they lifted their game and soon snuffed out England's challenge—after conceding the first try.

None was more inspired than Brownlie's brother, Maurice. He helped create a try for the All Black winger Snowy Svenson with one of his many powerful charges and during the second spell scored one himself, carrying England players over the line in his supercharged fury.

Wing forward Jim Parker and winger Jack Steel also scored tries, allowing New Zealand to establish a commanding 17–3 lead. It was sufficient cushion against a late rally by England which produced a penalty goal and a converted try.

The Brownlie brothers will be forever linked with this match. But there was another crucial episode, almost as controversial in English eyes as the Brownlie ordering-off.

The All Blacks' strongly-built winger Steel made a superb run down the touchline for a try to give his side the lead at 6–3. England's players and supporters claimed he had put a foot in touch during his run but the touch judge, a former New Zealand test referee Len Simpson, was adamant he hadn't and the try stood.

Maurice Brownlie powers through a maze of English defenders to score his famous try at Twickenham in 1925—40 minutes after his older brother Cyril had been ordered off.

ENGLAND
v.
NEW ZEALANDERS
AT TWICKENHAM.
Saturday, 3rd Jan., 1925
Kick-off 2.30 p.m.

WEST STAND
Block M
NOTE—Entrance to Ground in Whitton Road
Entrance to Seats at BACK of Stand.
Row 8   Seat 120
Price - 10/-

Eng. Commdr., R.N., Secretary R.F.U.

THE IMPOSSIBLE VICTORY

18 August 1976—Ellis Park, Johannesburg
New Zealand 32 Quagga-Barbarians 31

The secret to successful captaincy is to remain cool under pressure. Andy Leslie certainly demonstrated that quality when the All Blacks took on a star-studded Quagga-Barbarians team at Ellis Park during their long tour of South Africa in 1976.

There wasn't an awful lot Leslie (or any other captain) could have said when the All Blacks, coming off a thrilling test victory against the Springboks, found themselves down 31–9 with just over 20 minutes to play.

'I told the boys to forget about any pre-match instructions and just do their best,' said Leslie. 'It seemed to be a case of making the best out of a bleak situation.' 'Doing their best' would bring about an astonishing transformation. A mix of desperation, inventiveness and probably an element of relaxation among the opposition saw the All Blacks score 19 points in about as many minutes.

There were tries by Terry Mitchell, Alan Sutherland and Laurie Knight, and three goals from Laurie Mains while the Quagga-Barbarians were kept scoreless.

Now the scoreboard read 28–31 and the crowd—all 49,000 of them, a massive mid-week attendance—who'd probably been feeling sorry for the tourists, became riveted.

As the Quagga-Barbarians brought the ball back to halfway for the restart following Knight's try, skipper Leslie asked referee Steve Strydom how long there was to play.

'Twenty-nine seconds,' was his reply. Leslie, determined not to panic his players, went to them and assured them there were three minutes remaining.

From the restart, the ball went into touch off an All Black player. There were now only 10 to 15 seconds remaining . . . and it was a Quagga-Barbarians throw-in. Inevitably, they won possession and delivered the ball to flyhalf Gavin Cowley, an exciting, attacking player who searched for a path through to the goalposts.

Momentarily, it seemed he was en route to his team's fifth try of the afternoon but the defence held. Then Quaggas skipper Salty du Rand emerged from the mêlée and threw a giant pass towards his backs.

If they'd ever received it, the Quaggas had the numbers to score. But Leslie, anticipating brilliantly, seized the opportunity to intercept. He was away upfield but didn't fancy his chances of outrunning the opposition speedsters over 80 metres, so he kicked ahead.

It was a perfect kick, rolling end over end, taunting the Quaggas defenders who were trying to bring it under control. The All Blacks toed the ball on. Finally, at the 22 Quagga fullback Ian Robertson secured the ball and prepared to kick, knowing the instant the ball went across the touchline the game would be over.

Ian Robertson never did get his kick in, and was instead gunned down by his namesake, All Black centre Bruce Robertson. The ball rolled free. All eight All Black forwards were there to charge into the ruck, out from the Quagga-Barbarians posts.

All Black halfback Lyn Davis, in his haste to clear the ball, rolled his pass along the ground and almost had it intercepted. But it found its target, Duncan Robertson, who fired it on. Two more rapid passes and it was in the hands of winger Terry Mitchell who darted over unopposed to score in the corner.

Terry Mitchell across for the first of his two tries against the Quagga-Barbarians
in 1976. The second clinched an unlikely victory for the All Blacks.

The Moments

RUGBY WOULD NEVER have become the national game of New Zealand if its devotees had concerned themselves only with the deadly earnest business of winning matches. Winning is an important element, of course, particularly at the highest level and the stirring successes of the All Blacks throughout the century just finished has brought this tiny nation status, pride and a feel-good mentality.

But the reason rugby has become such a vital commodity in the nation's make-up relates to so much more than the outcome of matches, even though at the time tens of thousands of New Zealanders regard internationals (particularly against traditional foe like the Springboks) as life-and-death affairs.

Go to any rural community in New Zealand on a Saturday (or sometimes Sunday) afternoon and you'll more than likely find the rugby club the focal point of the entire community, the netball courts adjoining the rugby club, the club itself a virtual crèche for the district's children.

That's heartland rugby and it's the entire fabric of the game that sustains and inspires those communities, not just the most recent performance by the national team.

Which is the cue for this chapter on Moments, an intriguing pot-pourri of rugby happenings spread over more than a century, from the 1870s, when the greatest challenge facing officials in the capital was to locate a ground on which a match could be staged, through to 1998 when, a few months apart, the New Zealand women claimed a World Cup and the New Zealand sevens team lined up for the gold medal presentation at Kuala Lumpur.

There's the story of the incredible Native tour of the UK in 1888 and similar tales of the bizarre relating to the trail-blazing tour by the 1905 Originals.

There are portraits of a Ranfurly Shield match played in the snow in 1939 and of games, at Wellington in 1961 and Llanelli in 1989, that full-strength hurricanes failed to curtail.

And that's not all. Documented also are the occasions when 30 spectators attended a Springbok test, when radio and television came to rugby and how the Cavaliers defied the authorities.

As rugby chapters go, it is, to be sure, something completely different!

EARLY DAYS

When rugby was 'an excuse for anarchy and violence'

Athletic Park, headquarters of Wellington rugby for almost a century, and the scene of many famous contests, ceased to exist as a sporting stadium as the millennium came to a close.

In January 2000 the demolition gangs moved in, dismantling the grand old stadium. Within a few months a retirement home would begin to appear where the once famous rugby matches were played.

The new site for Wellington rugby fans, of course, is the handsome Westpac Trust Stadium on railway land in Thorndon Quay.

As famous a landmark as Athletic Park has been, it has to be recorded that the first representative rugby match to be played in Wellington predated the ground by more than three decades.

Back in 1870, even though rugby barely existed in New Zealand, the game was already important enough for trade to be interrupted. By then, the first game had been played in Nelson, the sport touching the imagination and enthusiasm of the locals.

That first recorded match under the then rules of rugby had taken place in May 1870 between Nelson College and the Nelson Football Club.

Word of this had reached Wellington and it was agreed that the capital would put up a team for a game against a Nelson side. The first problem was to get the South Islanders across Cook Strait.

Fortunately, Julius Vogel, who was later to become prime minister, ordered a cargo ship to be diverted to Nelson to bring the team across to Wellington.

Once the Nelson side was in the capital a venue was needed. C. J. (Charles) Monro, the man credited with introducing rugby to New Zealand and who, as Nelson's team manager, had organised the first game in Nelson, was in Wellington ahead of the team and dedicated himself to finding a suitable ground.

He looked at the Basin Reserve. Nope, it was 'half under water,

a place for bittern and the stork'. He began a trek around Wellington, looking at grounds in Hobson and Te Aro, but both were too small.

So he hit out for the Hutt Valley, on foot. A farmer by the name of Lumsden offered one of his fields; the offer was accepted by Monro, who trekked back into town. He would write later, in 1932, that there was no traffic, that not a single conveyance passed him, allowing him the time and peace for a leisurely and comfortably 'cast along the road'.

By the time the Nelson team arrived, Lumsden's field had flooded. So it was off to Petone, where Monro found another field. This one was dry but dangerously stony. Even so, real men don't worry about such things.

The game got going. Deep in the game, the Nelson lads were noticeably tiring, but still confident. They had good reason for this—the Nelson management had had a major hand in selecting the Wellington team! On Nelson rolled to a victory by three goals to nil.

Not everyone appreciated the physical nature of rugby back in the nineteenth century. In 1875, a Dunedin paper had claimed rugby as 'nothing more than an excuse for anarchy and violence'.

The same year a Wanganui paper homed in on spectators being 'heard giving voice to their feelings of contempt'.

And in 1887, after Frederick Pilling died from spinal damage suffered playing rugby, the coroner recorded: 'The game of rugby is only worthy of savages.'

Even the Wellington Rugby Union's minutes ruefully noted, 'Somehow, rugby has got a bad name and a large section of the public are never done condemning it. It is brutal, it is coarse, it is not scientific.'

Above: *The Wellington Club team which met Nelson Combined Clubs at Wellington, on 15 August 1873. The result was a draw, with two tries to each side.*

Right: *C. J. (Charles) Monro, the man credited with introducing rugby to New Zealand and who managed the Nelson team to Wellington in 1870.*

BOK BUSTERS

*After 70 years of trying
the All Blacks finally win a test series in South Africa*

Winning rugby's World Cup in 1987 had been special for the All Blacks. But defeating the Springboks on South African soil for the first time, in 1996, might just have matched it in terms of sheer achievement and satisfaction.

The triumph over the Springboks probably held greater significance for famous former internationals like Fred Allen, Sid Going and Brian Lochore.

'I think I might have shed a tear when the boys finally achieved what was for New Zealand the last remaining challenge in rugby,' said Allen whose team had been whitewashed in South Africa in 1949. Going said after the frustrations of 1970 and 1976—when the All Blacks had had to contend with South African referees as well as powerful opponents—it was marvellous to finally break through. Lochore found the series victory was especially sweet for those who'd been involved in the World Cup disappointment in South Africa the previous year. 'I know how intensely disappointed the players were after losing that epic contest in extra time. But they rose from the ashes and triumphed.'

The five previous series in South Africa—in 1928, 1949, 1960, 1970 and 1976—had all involved four internationals, with New Zealand's best return being way back in '28, when Maurice Brownlie's men shared the spoils. In '49, Fred Allen's men suffered a humiliating whitewash while the team's of '60, '70 and '76 could manage no more than a solitary test victory.

Because the 1996 series involved only three tests—the advent of the Tri-nations championship in the same year meaning New Zealand and South Africa would actually clash five times—winning the first international was absolutely vital.

So there was delight in the All Black camp when they held on to defeat their great rivals 23–19 at King's Park in Durban, a match in which Zinzan Brooke made the difference. He brought off countless thumping tackles, provided the deft little flick-on pass that created Christian Cullen's try and, fittingly, scored the clincher himself. The second test at Loftus Versfeld in Pretoria was another triumph for the multi-talented Brooke. He scored another try, drop-kicked a goal and stopped the Springbok forwards' rhinoceros charge in the final seconds of an enthralling and physically demanding contest. The 31-year-old Brooke was one of the few All Black forwards with enough energy to still be standing when French referee Didier Mene signalled the end of this memorable encounter. Most of his fellow forwards were strewn on the turf, near exhaustion, their energies utterly spent.

Sean Fitzpatrick, the captain, took nearly a minute to get to his feet. He'd played himself to a standstill. 'When I saw the Springboks readying for that last tap penalty, I wondered if collectively we had enough energy left to stop them. I believe it was the most physically sapping game I have ever been involved in.'

The All Blacks appeared to be breezing to victory at 24–11 but the South Africans defiantly clawed their way up to 23–24 with 19 minutes to play. Then it became a war of attrition.

Two penalty goals coolly slotted by replacement first-five Jon Preston and a snappy dropped goal by the incomparable Brooke gave the All Blacks a seven-point buffer which, under the most intense pressure, they defended until the finish.

That the final international, at Ellis Park in Johannesburg, was lost 32–22 mattered not—the All Blacks had finally beaten the odds and won on South African soil.

Already at 6000 feet and wanting to go higher, the All Blacks of 1996 chase possession against the Springboks at Pretoria. A victory in this game secured an historic first series victory on South African soil.

'BUGGER'

A six-letter word that shocked the nation

On 1 September 1956, the All Blacks beat the Springboks at Eden Park 11–5 to win the series. Just after the match the giant forward Peter Jones stepped up to a microphone to make one of the shortest and most sensational speeches in New Zealand rugby history.

Jones was one of the All Blacks' leading heroes in that match after he charged away from a lineout and collected the loose ball to run more than 30 metres for the side's only try.

In those days it was rare for any player, even those who might have played well, to be quoted by the media after the match and it was equally uncommon for anyone other than a captain to address the crowd.

But this was a special occasion—the first time the All Blacks had taken a series from their arch-rivals—and so Jones was called up to take the microphone by the ground announcer, Colin Snedden.

Still in a state of euphoria and confusion, Jones said, 'I never want to play a game like that again. I'm absolutely buggered.'

Not only did the thousands in front of the Eden Park grandstand erupt in mirth but so did countless others throughout New Zealand who were huddled around their radios, listening to Winston McCarthy's incomparable match commentary. It was a broadcast the country would have been tuned to and in those days would have been matched only by a Melbourne Cup race broadcast or a state of the nation address from the Prime Minister.

In the late 1990s the word 'bugger' has become almost socially and even legally acceptable, the theme indeed of an amusing television advertisement for Toyota. But in the 1950s it was considered obscene.

A memo was issued by the NZBC prohibiting the recording from being played on radio again. The tape was locked securely away and was not used again until Dunedin broadcaster Peter Sellers used it in a documentary programme in the 1980s.

Such was Jones's heroism that his momentary lapse was quickly forgiven though not quite forgotten.

For that generation of New Zealanders born before the early 1950s there has never been another year quite like that of 1956. That year New Zealand, also at Eden Park, won its first cricket test, beating the West Indies, and the Olympic Games were held in nearby Melbourne.

But the Springboks' tour and the series win by the All Blacks was the main preoccupation then and has provided the most enduring memory since. Rarely has rugby fever gripped the nation as it did that year when it became almost a national crusade to right the imagined wrongs of the 1937 and 1949 All Blacks series losses against the Springboks.

All the passion and emotion that went into that year's rugby was encapsulated in the Jones try and of course the Jones speech.

Peter Jones hurtles for the goalposts and the try that would seal the All Blacks' status as unofficial world champions.

Inset: *Jones later told the crowd exactly how he felt!*

"EYE-WITNESS" ACCOUNT OF THE FOURTH TEST —

NEL FLUKES THE KICK-OFF —

CLARKE KICKS A PENALTY! —

JONES SCORES A TRY! —

CLARKE ANOTHER PENALTY! —

WHITE'S INJURED —

DRYBURGH A TRY —

THE END! WE'VE WON! —

WELL, AT LEAST WE HEARD PETER JONES' SPEECH

THE ORIGINALS

The tour that transformed a bunch of colonials into the mighty All Blacks

A favourite image of the All Blacks' 1905–06 tour of Britain and France is of fullback-wing Billy Wallace attempting a conversion while wearing a sun hat.

In the side's match against Cornwall he even had the hat on when he scored a try. But don't think for one minute that those All Blacks were in any way casual or frivolous.

The 1905–06 All Blacks, of which Wallace was one of the brightest stars, have become one of the most important teams not only in rugby history but also in New Zealand's social history. In their own way they helped refine our sense of national identity.

The side became known as 'The Originals'. It was the first completely national team to undertake a major tour of Britain and it was during that tour that the name the All Blacks was adopted. The success of that tour has been one of the early reasons why the game has become so much part of the country's psyche.

In several other ways the Originals were trail-blazers. They were probably the first rugby side that made the game something of a science. In their captain, Dave Gallaher, and vice captain, Billy Stead, they had two master tacticians. Among their many innovations—unheard of at the turn of the century but standard practice today—were code names for planned moves, the use of skip passes to create uncertainty and the belief that possession, speed to breakdowns and backing up were essential.

Their thorough planning and balanced all-round game were reflected in their record. Of 35 games played, 34 were won and 976 points amassed with only 59 conceded. Wallace and other backs like wing Duncan McGregor and centre Jimmy Hunter were pro-

lific scorers. They, along with players such as Charles Seeling and Gallaher, became legends.

Even the one game they lost—0–3 against Wales—has become celebrated. It appears the referee erred in not awarding a try to the three-quarter Bob Deans. On his deathbed, just four years later, Deans is said to have insisted he did ground the ball legitimately over the line.

The side's aura endures and in the 1990s the team was admitted to the country's sports hall of fame without a word of dissent.

Just how the title All Blacks came to be fitted to New Zealand's national rugby team remains a matter for conjecture. The most popular theory is that during the Originals' tour a correspondent had copy that he phoned to his newspaper misinterpreted. Greatly impressed that the forwards could play as speedily and effectively as their counterparts in the backline, he referred to the New Zealanders as 'all backs' which was misprinted in the newspaper (and on placards) as 'All Blacks'.

Rod Chester and Nev McMillan in their monumental work *Men in Black* record that the first time the name appeared in print was in the *Daily Mail* following the team's 63–0 win over Hartlepool Clubs, the eighth game of the tour. Rugby correspondent J. A. Buttery, in a glowing report on the tourists' performance, wrote: 'The All Blacks, as the colonials are known.' Earlier in the tour he had referred to the New Zealanders as 'The Blacks'.

What we do know is that before the mighty 1905 team set sail for the UK they were simply New Zealanders but when they returned they were the All Blacks.

Billy Wallace lands a conversion during the All Blacks' 1905 tour of the UK. It was indicative of the attacking qualities of the Originals that Wallace landed 74 conversions during the tour but only three penalty goals.
Inset: Dave Gallaher.

BOK ODDITIES

Two bizarre tales of the 1981 Springboks

The Game That Never Was

Twenty-eight thousand fans packed into Hamilton's Rugby Park, eager to see whether their beloved Waikato team, holder of the Ranfurly Shield, could emulate its predecessor of 1956 and knock over the Springboks.

They are still wondering because the game never started. Some 15 minutes before the scheduled 2 p.m. kick-off, more than 400 protesters (part of a group of about 3000 who had marched from the city centre) broke down the fence at the north end of the ground and invaded the playing field.

Despite appeals by Commissioner of Police Bob Walton to move away, the protesters stayed put until eventually it was announced that the game was abandoned. Walton had ordered the protesters to be arrested, one by one, a laborious process as two policemen were needed to remove each individual.

Walton's decision to order the abandonment of the game was influenced by a report that a light plane, stolen from Taupo, was heading towards Hamilton on a 'kamikaze' mission.

The outcome was a heartbreak for the Waikato players who, with All Blacks Bruce Smith, Arthur Stone, John Boe, Brian Morrissey, John Fleming, Hud Rickit and Paul Koteka in the side, were confident of a bold showing.

The balance of the Springbok tour was considered in jeopardy as a result of the Hamilton pitch invasion, but in the event the remaining 13 matches were played. The game against the Hanan Shield Districts team, in Timaru, was cancelled two weeks out to allow the police to give their overworked troops much-needed rest.

The Smallest Test Turnout

After the trauma of their New Zealand visit, the Springboks were probably eager to return home, but before then they had three further matches, including a test, scheduled in the United States.

The first two of these encounters, at Wisconsin and Albany, were completed satisfactorily but the build-up of protest action meant that the venue and kick-off time for the test was kept secret.

The game was scheduled for a Saturday but on the Friday decoy groups were sent out, including a quarter of the Springbok touring party who went to a tourist attraction. Once the diversion had been created, the two teams made their way to a polo ground at Glenville, some 45 minutes away from Albany.

Such was the secrecy surrounding the event that a mere 30 spectators—most of them bemused local residents who knew nothing about rugby—looked on as South Africa and the United States engaged each other at test level for the first time. Seventy-five New York state policemen circled the ground.

Ed Hagerty, editor of the American *Rugby* magazine and one of the few journalists who witnessed the bizarre event, wrote that 'despite the lack of spectators, the game was as intense as if it were played before a packed house, and the action was spectacular.'

The South African media only found out about the game when the players returned to their hotel!

For the record, the Springboks won the game 38–7 after conceding the first try and holding a modest half-time lead of 6–4. Ray Mordt completed his second hat-trick of tries in successive tests, having touched down three times against the All Blacks at Eden Park. The other winger Gerrie Germishuys scored two tries.

It wasn't Waikato or the Springboks who won at Rugby Park, Hamilton, in 1981 but the protesters.
A pitch invasion by 400 prevented the match from starting.

THE WORLD CUP IS OURS!

The 1987 All Blacks rate as one of the greatest teams of all time

The 1987 season will always be a landmark in New Zealand rugby history, one which emits a golden glow.

The All Blacks played with rare verve and confidence to sweep all before them in the inaugural World Cup, and after posting huge scores against Italy, Fiji and Argentina in pool play, Scotland in the quarter-finals and Wales in the semi-finals, beat France 29–9 in the final at Eden Park.

It was a tonic which had been desperately needed. Just the year before, with controversy over contacts with South Africa coming to a sensational climax, New Zealand rugby had been plunged into deep despair. Divisions over the unauthorised Cavaliers' tour to South Africa and the replacement of suspended test stalwarts by what became known as the Baby Blacks caused a disunity which contributed to a 2–1 series loss to the Wallabies and a heavy defeat to France at Nantes.

But the pain of 1986 was rewarded by a reconstructed All Black side which in 1987 was superbly directed by a new coaching panel of Brian Lochore, Alex Wyllie and John Hart.

David Kirk (the stand-in captain for an injured Andy Dalton), John Kirwan, John Gallagher, Grant Fox, Wayne Shelford, Michael Jones (then an exciting, fresh discovery), Alan Whetton, Gary Whetton, Steve McDowell and Sean Fitzpatrick emerged as the playing stars.

But close behind were Craig Green, Joe Stanley, Warwick Taylor, Murray Pierce and John Drake. Add reserves like Terry Wright, Kieran Crowley, Frano Botica (who didn't even get on the field), Zinzan Brooke, Andy Earl and Richard Loe—and without argument the 1987 All Blacks rank as one of the greatest teams of all time.

And although the All Blacks' victory provided the crowning glory, the World Cup tournament itself, despite early reservations, proved to be an overwhelming success, rekindling a rugby fervour New Zealand hadn't experienced since the 1960s.

The tournament was shared with Australia and that was a weakness. The Wallabies, coached by controversial Alan Jones, didn't play to expectations and that affected that country's enthusiasm. But the semi-final between the Wallabies and France was one of the most thrilling ever played.

That the tournament became a reality was due to a joint New Zealand-Australian effort. In doing so, they had to overcome the usual British negativity. At the behest of the British, John Kendall-Carpenter was made tournament chairman. Unfortunately, he tended to be both patronising and interfering, and this led to many commercial and organisational shortcomings. Happily, most of these have since been remedied as even the British have realised the World Cup's huge potential.

David Kirk across for a try that helped New Zealand put away France in the final of the inaugural World Cup at Eden Park in 1987.

THE BIRTH OF TELEVISED RUGBY

NZRFU officials were reluctant to allow live telecasts

In recent years New Zealanders have become used to watching much of their top sport on television and this has given rise to a new breed of sporting addicts generally known as 'couch potatoes' or, as the Americans call them, 'Monday morning quarterbacks'.

But it wasn't always like this. For many years rugby authorities were steadfastly opposed to live telecasts of any matches.

This was one of rugby's most constant controversies since the advent of television in New Zealand around 1960 through to the 1970s. It was exceeded only in rancour and intensity by the arguments caused by contacts with South Africa because of that country's apartheid policy.

The NZRFU and its provinces were convinced that to allow live telecasts would have disastrous effects on attendances for major matches and on its revenue. Their argument was backed up by the fact that the, then, state-run television was fairly tight-fisted in what it offered by way of compensation.

NZRFU annual meetings through the sixties and into the seventies were often dominated by debates over the rights and wrongs of allowing live telecasts and the union's stubborn refusals to allow them caused much controversy and brought the union considerable criticism.

One of the few who saw that accommodating television was inevitable if the game wished to grow was J. J. Stewart, who was then NZRFU delegate for Wanganui. Gradually, the most conserva-

tive of the union's hierarchy came around to his view and in 1972 the NZRFU finally agreed to live telecasts.

The first rugby match to be telecast live nationally was the Wallabies' clash with Hawkes Bay in 1972. The fact only 9000 turned up gave strength to those who claimed televised play kept the fans at home.

The first test televised live was New Zealand's game against Australia at Eden Park that same season. As 43,000 attended, it could be claimed TV had no impact on that fixture. In addition to the massive nationwide audience, the NZRFU also received $8750 for the television rights.

Yet it wasn't only rugby's administration that was tardy in recognising the popularity of live telecasts. The then Broadcasting Corporation was initially reluctant to use the new satellite feed for the first live telecast from abroad—New Zealand's international against Wales at Cardiff in late 1972.

Another landmark telecast was the 1975 'water polo' test between the All Blacks and Scotland at Eden Park—the first live test in colour.

It's amazing how quickly rugby in New Zealand has changed. Indeed, because of the deal struck with the Murdoch empire in 1995 to allow professionalism, television probably now has more control over the way top rugby is run than the game's administrators.

Phil Bennett's fateful final kick at Cardiff in 1972—the first test telecast live into New Zealand from overseas. The kick missed, allowing the All Blacks to beat Wates 19–16.

BLACK FERNS WIN THE WORLD CUP

Vanessa was a star—after nearly missing the plane

It's hard to say which was the greater achievement in women's rugby in 1998—the New Zealand girls blitzing every opponent as they claimed the World Cup in Amsterdam or Vanessa Cootes scoring five tries in the final.

A New Zealand victory was probably the more predictable because the Black Ferns—as they would become known—had dominated the women's scene for several seasons. But Cootes, the individual star of New Zealand's crushing 44–12 win over the United States in the final, was fortunate to be on the plane to Amsterdam.

Cootes had burst on to the rugby scene in 1995 at the age of 25, the wonder winger from Hamilton making an astonishing impact by scoring four tries against Australia in her national debut.

With a massive haul of nine tries against France in 1996 and those five cherished touchdowns in the World Cup final, she claims an astonishing record of 35 tries from just 10 test appearances!

Amazingly, up until the winter of 1995, when Cootes first pulled on the black jersey, she'd never played footie in her life. It was only when her sister (who happened to play club rugby in Hamilton) rang her up one afternoon to say her team was a player short that Cootes even considered it.

Until then, she'd been content playing touch—at which she'd represented New Zealand—and representative softball and netball. She'd actually had plans to fill in her Saturday afternoons by playing soccer.

A year later she was holding up the trophy as the New Zealand women's player of the year and in 1996 also became New Zealand's first female professional rugby player when she signed to play for Lyon in France.

Although the signing was a landmark for New Zealand women's rugby, ultimately it was to cost Cootes as a player. Although her obvious goal was to represent New Zealand at the World Cup in 1998, she nearly blew it when she returned from France with serious ligament damage to her knee and having stacked on weight.

At the World Cup trials, it was clear she'd lost her blistering pace and she was no longer the selectors' first-choice winger. Instead, the selectors pencilled in Louisa Wall, Diane Kahura, Cheryl Waaka and Shannon Andrew. Cootes, struggling for form, looked like she was going to miss the plane.

But then Andrew broke her collar bone in a sevens game and Cootes came into the squad as a replacement. She was left on the sidelines as the Black Ferns opened their World Cup campaign but then she played against Scotland, was stood down for the quarter-final clash against Spain, and reintroduced for the semi-final against England.

It was the turning point. She was harder, stronger, tougher than before, both mentally and physically, and she met the English head on, bursting through the middle with new-found power thanks to the upper-body strength she had built up while recovering from her knee injury. She turned in a blinder, scoring two stunning tries and playing her way into the final. The rest, as they say, is history.

The New Zealand girls scored a staggering 59 tries in five outings while conceding just three. They were in such command that they only needed to kick two penalty goals. They defeated Germany 134–6 and Scotland 76–0 in pool play, Spain 46–3 in a quarter-final, England 44–11 in a semi-final and the USA 44–12 in the final.

Playing a spectacular brand of rugby, they so captured the public's imagination that four times as many New Zealanders watched their final live on television as watched the Arsenal-Newcastle FA Cup final.

---

124   *Vanessa Cootes—try-scorer extraordinaire. She's bagged 35 tries in 10 tests, including five in the World Cup final.*

HARD LUCK STORIES

For some the Shield has meant heartbreak and anguish

For some of New Zealand's provincial unions, a significant contribution to their tradition and heritage has been either long reigns with the Ranfurly Shield or unexpected wins against the odds.

But for some unions the Shield has meant only heartbreak and anguish, providing a harsh reminder that in sport losing is as much a reality as is winning.

Two unions at the top of that hard-luck list are Counties and Wanganui, who by the turn of the century had never experienced the joy of winning New Zealand rugby's most famous trophy.

On any number of occasions each has been heart-breakingly close. Wanganui and its strongly-built winger Colin Pierce (whose son Scott would become an All Black trialist) will never forget the two heart-breaking Shield challenges against Taranaki in the early 1960s.

Pierce was the individual star of both games. In 1963 he kicked four penalty goals to give Wanganui a 12–11 lead going into the final minute when replacement wing Kerry Hurley chip-kicked ahead, got a favourable bounce, and amid frantic sideline scenes scored in the corner to provide Taranaki with a 14–12 win.

One year later Pierce again landed four penalty goals. Then, in the last minute he scored a try to level the scores at 15–all. Unfortunately for Pierce, he hooked the conversion, allowing Taranaki to escape once again.

Just as Pierce will be remembered as Wanganui's most glorious Shield loser, the Counties' failures will be identified in the same perverse way with one of that union's most distinguished players, All Black hooker and captain Andy Dalton.

Between 1975 and 1985, virtually the span of Dalton's representative career, Counties made seven challenges, with Dalton as captain in the last six. The results were all agonisingly close: 6–7 versus Auckland in 1975, 10–15 versus Manawatu in 1977, 9–11 versus Auckland in 1979, 20–20 versus Waikato in 1981, 15–15 versus Canterbury in 1982, 19–27 versus to Canterbury in 1984 and 9–12 versus to Auckland in 1985.

In those seven matches in which Dalton was involved Counties was outscored by only 107 points to 88. But in subsequent recollections Dalton was rankled only by two of those games. The first was the 1982 draw with Canterbury when Robbie Deans kicked a late penalty goal for a questionable backline offside. The other game was the 1985 defeat against Auckland, when Dalton along with all the Counties players was convinced loose forward Dave Trombik clearly scored a try that was disallowed.

Another unlucky challenger has been Bay of Plenty. On two occasions it effectively had the Shield won only to witness miraculous escapes by the holder.

In 1922 in a game against Hawkes Bay at Hastings a late try beside the goalposts brought Bay of Plenty up to 16–17. The taker of the conversion began 'shaking like a leaf' and missed the kick. The Shield would remain with Hawkes Bay for another five years.

And in 1996 Bay of Plenty journeyed to Eden Park for a challenge against Auckland, whose All Blacks were away in South Africa. When the Bay led 29–11 with 10 minutes remaining, preparations were under way in Rotorua for a heroes' welcome home. But Auckland managed three late tries, including a wide-angle conversion from Matt Carrington, to win the game 30–29.

Kent Lambert gets his marching orders from referee Colin Gregan at Palmerston North in 1977.
Even with 14 men Manawatu hung on to defeat Counties.
Inset: *The programme from Counties' luckless Shield challenge at Eden Park in 1985.*

NEW ZEALAND STRIKES GOLD AT KL

New Zealand was always favoured once Lomu, Cullen and Vidiri were released

Rugby has featured four times at the Olympic Games—in 1900 at Paris (France winning the gold medal), in 1908 at London (when Australia was successful), and in 1920 at Antwerp and 1924 at Paris (with the United States coming out on top both times). These are sobering results to recall because they mean the United States can claim to be the reigning Olympic rugby champion!

Although New Zealand was among the strongest rugby nations in the world then, it never despatched a side to any of those Games because of the horrendous amount of travel—let alone cost—involved. (It would have taken a full month on a boat, both ways, just to get to Europe.)

The United States may very well remain the Olympic rugby champion forever because if rugby is ever accepted back into the Games—and the International Rugby Board continues to lobby the IOC—almost certainly the game that will be played is sevens, not the traditional 15-a-side version.

It was sevens that featured at Kuala Lumpur in 1998 when host nation Malaysia decided to introduce rugby to the Commonwealth Games for the first time. Obviously, the USA and France didn't feature since they were not Commonwealth countries. That left Australia—with evergreen David Campese involved—as the only nation eligible to complete the historic Olympic-Commonwealth rugby double. But Fiji shattered those hopes by downing Campo's men in the semi-finals.

The gold medals this time would go to the New Zealanders, brilliantly prepared by sevens' coaching maestro Gordon Tietjens. Notwithstanding Fiji's World Cup triumph and their continuing domination of the abbreviated version of rugby, the New Zealanders were always favourites from the moment the NZRFU agreed to release All Blacks Jonah Lomu, Christian Cullen and Joeli Vidiri from their NPC commitments.

Lomu emerged as the individual star of the medal-winning performance, although Tietjens admits he was worried about Jonah's fitness when the players first assembled.

At Kuala Lumpur Lomu missed only the second half of the opening encounter against Sri Lanka, remaining on the field throughout New Zealand's other six matches. He grabbed a hat-trick of tries in the quarter-final against Wales, set up Roger Randle for a crucial try in the tense semi-final against Samoa and was the commanding individual in the classic final, won 21–12 against Fiji.

In the final he was astonishing, swiping king-sized opponents aside with giant fends, running down speedster Rauqe from behind and creating tries for Dallas Seymour and Christian Cullen.

To qualify top and thus remain on the opposite side of the draw to Fiji, the New Zealanders needed to score 15 tries against the Bahamas in the final qualifying match. 'I told them to play at 100 miles an hour,' said Tietjens. They did, winning 93–0—an astonishing result in a 14-minute game.

There were intensely emotional scenes at the finish—Lomu shedding tears and being endlessly hugged and kissed by his captain Eric Rush (who had been under an injury cloud until 24 hours before the tournament started). The New Zealanders performed at least three hakas for the admiring crowd before fronting up for the medal ceremony.

Dallas Seymour and Jonah Lomu, two of the stars of New Zealand's gold medal-winning sevens team at the Kuala Lumpur Commonwealth Games.

A CAVALIER TOUR

The rebel Cavalier tour was a masterpiece of covert planning

The All Blacks wanted to undertake a full-scale tour of South Africa in 1985 but two Auckland lawyers, Paddy Finnegan and Philip Recordon, scuttled it by filing an injunction with the High Court, claiming the tour was not in the best interests of New Zealand.

The High Court upheld their claim, denying New Zealand's leading players the opportunity to pit their skills against their great foe, the Springboks. The cancellation devastated individuals like coach Brian Lochore and left the players seething.

A substitute tour of Argentina was no consolation at all—a game against the Pumas is no more than a preamble to a series clash with the mighty Springboks—so plans were secretly put in place to undertake a rebel tour of the Republic in 1986.

It was a masterpiece of covert planning, the entire operation being shrouded in secrecy until a few days before the players assembled in South Africa. Even then, many usually well-informed pundits thought it was a smokescreen, that a handful of individuals had been invited to the Republic to represent a World XV. In the organisers' favour was the fact that a number of All Blacks had been in the UK participating in the England Union's centenary celebrations. They flew directly to South Africa.

Remarkably, 28 of the 30 players originally selected to tour featured on the Cavaliers tour. Unavailable were John Kirwan and David Kirk, their places being taken by Bernie Fraser and Andrew Donald. Manager Dick Littlejohn and coach Lochore declined to be involved and their substitutes were Ian Kirkpatrick and Colin Meads.

Grant Fox would write in his autobiography *The Game, The Goal*: 'Every one of us had rugby at heart. Every one of us believed rugby, the game, had been dealt an injustice. For New Zealanders, the greatest challenge in rugby remained the defeat of South Africa in South Africa. We had been deprived even of confronting that challenge, let alone beating the Springboks.'

The original 1985 itinerary comprised 16 matches with three internationals, all generously spaced. What the Cavaliers accepted was little short of rugby suicide—12 matches in six weeks with four internationals on successive Saturdays and games against each of South Africa's strongest provinces.

The challenge, daunting enough, became even harder when Burger Geldenhuys slugged Cavaliers captain Andy Dalton in the second match, breaking his jaw. The hapless All Black leader would take no further part in the tour (being replaced by John Mills).

Although the Cavaliers produced some memorable moments they were outflanked by the Springboks in the tests. Like the All Blacks of 1970 and 1976, they dropped the series 3–1. The Springboks won the first test in Cape Town 21–15, the third test in Pretoria 33–18 and the fourth test in Johannesburg 24–10 while the Cavaliers took out the second test in Durban 19–18.

The individual who broke the hearts of the New Zealanders was flyhalf Naas Botha who accounted for 69 of the Springboks' 96 points, although he let the Cavaliers off the hook at Durban by missing a last-gasp drop-kick from directly in front.

In the provincial matches, the Cavaliers defeated a Griquas Invitation XV 22–21, Northern Transvaal 10–9, Orange Free State 31–9, Western Province 26–15, Natal 37–24, South African Barbarians 42–13 and Western Transvaal 26–18 while losing to Transvaal 19–24.

Upon their return to New Zealand, the players were handed a two-test suspension by the NZRFU, which also investigated allegations the players had been paid while on tour. Chairman Russ Thomas duly announced that because of insufficient evidence, all charges concerning payment to the players was dropped.

Not the All Blacks but the Cavaliers, who organised their own tour of South Africa in 1986, here relaxing at Mala Mala Game Reserve. At right are coach and manager Colin Meads and Ian Kirkpatrick.

THE NATIVE TOUR

The tour was the brainchild of English businessman Tom Eyton

When the 1888–89 New Zealand Native team set sail on the first major rugby tour from the Southern Hemisphere, it could not have realised that it would set the style for thousands of rugby tours and trips that would follow.

They were 26 New Zealanders (22 Maori and four Pakeha) whose world tour was to last 14 months and take in a grand total of 107 matches. The tour was the brainchild of English businessman Tom Eyton who lived in New Zealand. He had been home to England in 1887 and had wondered, when watching rugby there, what the reaction would be if he arranged for a team of New Zealanders to tour.

The Rugby Football Union was sceptical at first since it had no idea how New Zealanders played rugby. Yet Eyton persisted with his concept of an all-Maori touring team. He struck some problems due to insufficient Maori players being available but he was not perturbed—he simply invited four players who looked like Maori to make up the numbers.

Eyton took £62 off each man for his fare and the team departed New Zealand, but not before first touring the country, playing from north to south. First stop was Melbourne where they adapted to playing under the Australian rules format. Then began the long voyage to Britain with the players taking turns to keep fit in the boiler room.

Once there, the team's schedule picked up at a crazy pace and was maintained through a whirlwind tour of all four home countries, resulting in some incidents that have become classics.

When playing against Carlisle, the rain and sleet were so bad that in the second half the Natives backs wore raincoats! Arthur Warbrick, tired of people repeatedly asking him to show his massive calf muscles, sometimes rolled up a trouser leg to facilitate an easier view for the curious. Dick Tairoa often used to wave to the crowds as he ran along. Once he blew a kiss to the opposition full-back as he ran through. Before the game against Middlesex, at Lord Sheffield's estate, the lunch was so sumptuous and the serving of drinks so liberal that several members of the team were incapable of playing. Lord Sheffield further impeded the Natives by sending out servants at half-time with more champagne.

At one point the popular Natives played six games in eight days. One of the team, Davey 'Iron Man' Gage, appeared in 68 of the 74 games in Britain.

Internationals were played against England (lost 0–7), Wales (lost 0–5) and Ireland (won 13–4). In the end, the Natives headed homewards, having made many friends. But they kept active, dashing off a further 14 games in Australia, then staging another eight-game tour of New Zealand.

It is reported that when the team finally reached Auckland after the 107th game (78 of which had been won), the members did not want to break up and go their separate ways.

Reproduced from Keith Quinn's Encyclopedia of World Rugby.

There was never a tour quite like that undertaken by the New Zealand Native team of 1888—they played 107 matches over almost 14 months!

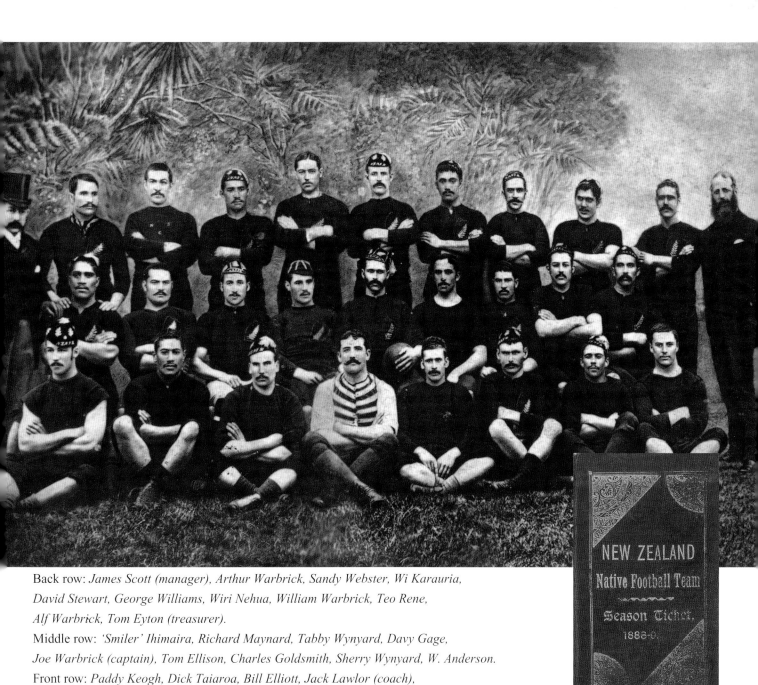

Back row: *James Scott (manager), Arthur Warbrick, Sandy Webster, Wi Karauria,*
David Stewart, George Williams, Wiri Nehua, William Warbrick, Teo Rene,
Alf Warbrick, Tom Eyton (treasurer).
Middle row: *'Smiler' Ihimaira, Richard Maynard, Tabby Wynyard, Davy Gage,*
Joe Warbrick (captain), Tom Ellison, Charles Goldsmith, Sherry Wynyard, W. Anderson.
Front row: *Paddy Keogh, Dick Taiaroa, Bill Elliott, Jack Lawlor (coach),*
Mac McCausland, Charles Madigan, Fred Warbrick, Harry Lee.

NEW ZEALAND
Native Football Team
Season Ticket,
1888-9.

ELSOM'S CONVERSION

'It's great what you can do after a few beers!'

One of the greatest sporting moments at Lancaster Park (now Jade Stadium) took place in moonlight, long after the crowds had departed—the embankment deserted.

In 1954, Otago challenged Canterbury for the Ranfurly Shield. A crowd of 30,000 witnessed one of the most dramatic finishes in Shield history. Behind 6–9 with only seconds remaining a last desperate attack put Derek Mayo, the Canterbury fullback, over in the corner for the equalising try.

The Shield secured, a delirious crowd surged onto the field and hoisted Mayo shoulder high. Unable to clear the field of the jubilant spectators, referee Doug Graham blew the whistle for full-time with the conversion not taken—Canterbury 9, Otago 9.

The chaotic scenes at Lancaster Park after Mayo scored his celebrated try were vividly captured by Terry McLean in his book *Great Days in New Zealand Rugby*:

'Every picture, so they say, tells a story. There is a picture, even now of referee Graham standing on the spot where Mayo scored. The clock on the scoreboard above him shows that 41 minutes of the second half have been played. He is waiting patiently for the kick at goal to be taken.

'But all over the field are thousands upon thousands of fanatical dervishes seizing Mayo, seizing Cantabrians, flinging them aloft, uttering word after word of praise about them and dancing with the ultimate joy.

'Mr Graham took a look at the crowd and the situation. He forgot about the kick. Forgot about everything, in fact, except a game in which, for the space of half an hour or more, men turned, if not into gods, at least into superhuman beings.'

Later that night, after a beer or three, some of the senior members of the Canterbury team decided it was time to take the conversion.

Buddy Henderson, who went on to total a then record 163 points in Shield matches, was not considered for such an important kick because he was wearing street shoes. Dennis Young, the hooker, wanted to take the kick but Alan Elsom, an All Black, claimed the right—his argument helped by the fact that he was the only one still dressed in rugby gear.

Elsom placed the ball near the 22-metre line and stepped forward to take the most important kick of his career.

'It never looked like missing,' remembers Elsom. 'It's great what you can do after a few beers. Forget all the nonsense about an historic draw—we won, all right; Canterbury 11, Otago 9!'

Later, Pat Vincent, the Canterbury captain, was to remark 'We can't leave our run any later than that.'

Late at night, when the moon was out, Canterbury's try was finally converted!

STORM WARNING!

Days when Wellington and Llanelli were at the eye of the storm

Major rugby matches have taken place in some dreadful weather. In 1939 the field was covered in snow for the Southland–Manawatu Ranfurly Shield match, and in 1975 players faced a waterlogged Eden Park pitch for the All Blacks-Scotland test. Blizzards, especially in the South Island, have also caused problems, on occasions leading to cases of hypothermia.

But by common consent, the most vile weather for any game involving New Zealanders comes down to a dead heat between the 1961 test match between the All Blacks and France at Athletic Park, and the tour match the 1989 All Blacks played against Llanelli.

Had they been games other than internationals there's not much doubt both would have been abandoned and indeed for both games that option was considered.

Yet each game contained surprising skill and heroism which in the Athletic Park match have become the stuff of legends. During that match there were wind gusts in Cook Strait of around 80 mph. By an unhappy coincidence this was the first time Athletic Park's Millard Stand was used for a major game. Few were prepared to risk sitting in its upper deck.

Proper rugby was well nigh impossible in a game won by the All Blacks 5–3. But the scores each side obtained were memorable.

The French, who otherwise had an unhappy tour but won many plaudits for their bravery in this match, opened the scoring with 15 minutes left when the centre Jean Pique broke and sent the wing Jean Dupuy racing nearly 40 metres into the teeth of the wind for a remarkable try.

The chances of France snatching an improbable win were dashed three minutes later when from a scrum near the line the attempted clearing kick of fullback Claude Lacaze was charged down by Kel Tremain. His try was followed by an extraordinary conversion by Don Clarke from wide out. Clarke directed his kick almost parallel with the 22, the wind eventually sweeping it between the uprights.

The wind was just as vicious for the 1989 match at Llanelli with gusts of about 120 mph being recorded at the nearby airport. Parts of the ground were judged too dangerous for spectators and the temporary commentary box occupied by Keith Quinn, Earle Kirton and their fellow TVNZ crew members blew away soon after they had vacated it.

Playing with the wind, the All Blacks led 7–0 at half-time from a Steve McDowell try and a penalty which Grant Fox somehow goaled.

Fears that that wasn't enough were soon removed when the All Black pack, superbly led by Wayne Shelford, absolutely shut the Llanelli side out, retaining possession almost throughout the second half. The only points in the spell were from an Andy Earl try but the Llanelli players became so frustrated that they infringed constantly and were penalised accordingly, so that the final penalty count was 20–3 to New Zealand. This only enraged the Llanelli fans further and they attacked the Scottish referee Ken McCartney after the game.

All Black winger Ralph Caulton tangles with the French during the 1961 Hurricane test at Athletic Park.

A COMMENTARY, (SPECTATOR-WISE) ON THE SECOND TEST —

DESPITE THE CONDITIONS MANY ROSE TO GREAT HEIGHTS —

THERE WAS SOME NICE STRAIGHT RUNNING —

AND NOT A FEW WENT "ON THE BLIND" —

AND THOUGH THE COVER DEFENCE DID NOT ALWAYS HOLD —

WITH FAST EVASIVE TACTICS —

BUT, IN THE END THE WEATHER PROVED TOO MUCH —

AND MANY FAILED TO FOLLOW UP —

THERE WERE TOO, SOME SPIRITED PASSING MOVES —

"MOST ROADS NORTH ARE BLOCKED — THE FERRY SAILING IS POSTPONED — WELLINGTON AIRPORT IS CLOSED — BECAUSE OF SLIPS ON THE MAIN TRUNK —"

AND MANY FAILED TO FINISH-OFF THEIR MOVEMENTS

WHITE-OUT

Invercargill folk woke to find a massive fall of snow had whitened their city

Some of the most astonishing photographs of any rugby game played in New Zealand were shot in August 1939, when in Invercargill a Ranfurly Shield match between Southland and Manawatu was played on a carpet of snow.

Overnight, Invercargill had been hit by its heaviest snowstorm in 13 years and although the falls had stopped in mid-morning, attempts to clear the ground were hampered because the trucks volunteer staff were using were cutting into the surface.

Southland officials, in fact, had resigned themselves to having to postpone the game. But when they put this option to Manawatu's manager Mr W. Gleeson, whose son Jack was to be an All Black coach in the 1970s, he startled them by insisting the game proceed.

In the event Southland won the match 17–3, outscoring the Manawatu side by four tries to nil. Surprisingly, the snow didn't make the match conditions as impossible as most might have imagined.

A contemporary newspaper report commented: 'After an uncertain beginning in which players were puzzled by the vagaries of the playing surface and the unresponsive behaviour of the ball the game developed into a remarkable exhibition of good rugby.'

Among those who played in the game for Southland was prop Les George, a 1938 All Black and later a national selector, and halfback

Charlie Saxton, who captained the 1945–46 Army's Kiwi team.

Saxton was surprised in later years that the game should still be causing so much interest. He pointed out that there had been no mud, slush or wind—conditions that often prove more difficult in which to play.

'That's one of the things you learn quickly,' he said. 'In rugby you learn to adapt to any conditions and play in them without complaint.'

George said the day had been calm and the ball had not been difficult to handle. 'In fact, once you warmed up it was almost pleasant,' he said.

An enduring puzzle is what prompted Manawatu to insist the game go ahead after Southland had suggested a postponement. George was one of those baffled, but believes he may have got the answer when after the match over a refreshing ale he quizzed his close friend and fellow All Black Rod McKenzie, who in his 123rd first-class match captained the Manawatu team.

According to George, McKenzie had told him that Manawatu had theorised that because it was the inferior team the snow could act as mud often does to level the respective sides. Manawatu believed that its chances of winning were better than what they might have been in normal conditions.

It takes more than 10 inches of snow to stop a Ranfurly Shield match from proceeding.
The occasion was Manawatu's challenge against Southland at Invercargill in 1939. Inset: *Charlie Saxton.*

1870 • First rugby match played in New Zealand (Nelson College v Nelson Club at Nelson).

1884 • First New Zealand team selected (organised from Dunedin it toured New South Wales, winning all nine matches) • Point-scoring system adopted: try—1 point; conversion—2 points; other goals—3 points.

1893 • The NZRFU votes to adopt a black jersey with a silver fern leaf as its official uniform • First New Zealand team selected under the auspices of the NZRFU. Tours Australia under the captaincy of Tom Ellison. The team wins 9 of 10 matches.

1894 • Revision of point-scoring system: try—3 points; conversion—2 points; penalty goal—3 points; dropped goal and goal from a mark—4 points.

1905 • Value of a goal from a mark reduced to 3 points • First visit by New Zealand to the UK. The originals, captained by Dave Gallaher, win 32 of their 33 matches, losing only to Wales. The title All Blacks is adopted during the tour. Billy Wallace's 246 points and Jimmy Hunter's 44 tries are records that still stand.

1921 • First tour of New Zealand by South Africa. They square the series with the All Blacks 1–1, with the final test drawn 0–0.

1928 • First All Black tour of South Africa. Led by Maurice Brownlie, the team squares the series 2–2.

1931 • Lord Bledisloe, Governor-General of New Zealand, presents the Bledisloe Cup for competition between New Zealand and Australia. The first contest for the trophy, at Eden Park, attracts only 15,000 spectators, New Zealand winning 20–13 • This is the last year in which the 2–3–2 scrum applies.

1972 • Value of the try increased to four points • First direct telecast of an All Black test (against Australia at Eden Park) • First direct telecast by satellite of a test (New Zealand against Wales at Cardiff).

1973 • Scheduled Springbok tour of New Zealand cancelled by the Labour Government.

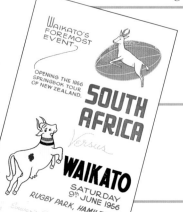

1981 • New Zealand becomes a divided country because of the Springbok tour.

1986 • The unauthorised Cavaliers undertake a full-scale tour of South Africa. All those involved are suspended for two tests upon their return • The Baby Blacks (minus Cavaliers) defeat France at Christchurch.

1995 • Third Rugby World Cup hosted by South Africa. The Springboks win the title, beating New Zealand after extra time in the final • After more than a century as an amateur game, the IRB declares rugby professional.

1996 • Super 12 and Tri-nations series introduced after Rupert Murdoch's News Corp injects $US550 million into the game. Auckland Blues and the All Blacks win the inaugural events.

1888 • *New Zealand Native team tours New Zealand, Australia and the UK, playing 107 matches.*

1892 • *NZRFU founded in Wellington.*

1902 • *Ranfurly Shield presented to the NZRFU by the Earl of Ranfurly, Governor of New Zealand. When the trophy arrives from the UK it features soccer goalposts and a round ball!*

1903 • *New Zealand's first test—against Australia at the Sydney Cricket Ground. The men in black, captained by Jimmy Duncan, win 22–3.*

1924 • *The All Blacks, captained by Cliff Porter, complete their 30-match tour of the UK and France undefeated, winning renown as The Invincibles.*

1926 • *First radio commentary of a rugby match by Alan Allardyce in Christchurch (the game Christchurch v HSOB).*

1948 • *Value of the dropped goal reduced to three points.*

1956 • *The All Blacks win a series against the Springboks for the first time, 3–1 in New Zealand.*

1976 • *National Provincial Championship (NPC) introduced.*

1978 • *All Blacks complete their first Grand Slam in the UK, defeating Ireland, Wales, England and Scotland.*

1987 • *First Rugby World Cup hosted by New Zealand, the All Blacks winning the Webb Ellis Trophy, defeating France in the final*

1992 • *Value of a try increased from four to five points.*

1996 • *All Blacks claim a series against the Springboks on South African soil for the first time • The Black Ferns win the Women's Rugby World Cup in The Netherlands.*

1999 • *Fourth Rugby World Cup hosted by Wales. Australia claims the crown, defeating France in the final after France whips New Zealand in the semi-finals.*

ILLUSTRATION ACKNOWLEDGEMENTS

Every effort has been made to trace the copyright owners of the material used in this book.
The author and publisher apologise for any omissions, and will be pleased to hear from those whom they were unable to trace.

The sources of the photographs and illustrations are listed below. Abbreviations: A= above; B= below; L= left; R= right; M= main picture; P= programme; Me= memorabilia; I= inset; AL= above left; C= centre; BR= below right.

Front cover: (Clockwise from top left) NZ Rugby Museum, NZ Rugby Museum, NZ Rugby Museum, Pro Sport Photos, John Selkirk, Pro Sport Photos, Pro Sport Photos, Photosport. *Back cover:* Me NZ Rugby Museum, M John Selkirk. *1* Photosport. *2–3* Photosport. *5* Rugby Southland. *6* (Clockwise from top left) NZ Rugby Museum, Pro Sport Photos, NZ Rugby Museum, Bob Howitt Collection, NZ Rugby Museum. *7* (Clockwise from top left) NZ Rugby Museum, Rugby Southland, News Media (Auckland), Neville Lodge Estate, NZ Rugby Museum, NZ Rugby Museum. *10* NZ Rugby Museum. *12* News Media (Auckland). *13* Bob Howitt Collection. *14* NZ Rugby Museum. *15* M NZ Rugby Museum, Me King Country Rugby Football Union. *16* News Media (Auckland). *17* John Selkirk. *18* L News Media (Auckland), R News Media (Auckland). *19* Photosport. *20* NZ Rugby Museum. *21* NZ Rugby Museum. *22* Frank Thompson/Crown Studios, Wellington. *23* M NZ Rugby Museum, Me NZ Rugby Museum. *24* NZ Rugby Museum. *25* NZ Rugby Museum. *26* News Media (Auckland). *27* Photosport. *28* News Media (Auckland). *29* Evening Post, Wellington/ Alexander Turnbull Library, 1956 Springboks 'A'. *30* Pro Sport Photos. *31* News Media (Auckland). *32* Pro Sport Photos. *33* Pro Sport Photos. *34* News Media (Auckland). *35* John Selkirk. *36* L Pro Sport Photos, R Pro Sport Photos. *37* John Selkirk. *38* NZ Rugby Museum. *39* The Dominion, Wellington. *40* News Media (Auckland). *41* M John Selkirk, Me NZ Rugby Museum. *42* The Dominion, Wellington. *42–3* NZ Rugby Museum. *43* Photosport. *44* NZ Rugby Museum. *45* NZ Rugby Museum. *46* News Media (Auckland). *47* Photosport. *48* M Photosport, Me NZ Rugby Museum. *49* NZ Rugby Museum. *50* Frank Thompson/Crown Studios, Wellington. *51* M NZ Rugby Museum, Me NZ Rugby Museum. *52* NZ Rugby Museum. *53* Fotopress. *54* News Media (Auckland). *55* News Media (Auckland). *56* John Selkirk. *56–7* News Media (Auckland). *57* Me NZ Rugby Museum, R News Media (Auckland). *58* Frank Thompson/Crown Studios, Wellington. *59* NZ Rugby Museum. *60* NZ Rugby Museum. *61* NZ Rugby Museum. *62* Pro Sport Photos. *63* Pro Sport Photos. *64* Pro Sport Photos. *65* Pro Sport Photos. *66* Photosport *67* Photosport. *68* News Media (Auckland). *69* Pro Sport Photos. *70* News Media (Auckland). *71* News Media (Auckland). *72* M News Media (Auckland), Me NZRFU. *73* News Media (Auckland). *74* NZ Rugby Museum. *75* NZ Rugby Museum. *76* News Media (Auckland). *79* M NZ Rugby Museum, Me Auckland Rugby Football Union. *81* Fotopress. *83* A NZ Rugby Museum, B NZ Rugby Museum. *85* M News Media (Auckland), Me NZ Rugby Museum. *87* Rhys Morris/Marlborough Publications Ltd. *89* M Lyndsay Knight/Rugby Press Ltd., Me NZ Rugby Museum. *91* News Media (Auckland). *93* Pro Sport Photos. *95* News Media (Auckland). *97* M Argus Printing and Publishing Company, Ltd. (S.A.), Me NZ Rugby Museum. *99* Otago Daily Times. *101* Fotopress. *103* New Zealand Herald. *105* M News Media (Auckland), Me NZ Rugby Museum. *107* M New Zealand Herald, Me NZ Rugby Museum. *108* NZ Rugby Museum. *111* A NZ Rugby Museum, B NZ Rugby Museum. *113* Fotopress. *114* Auckland Star. *115* M NZ Rugby Museum, I Neville Lodge Estate. *117* NZ Rugby Museum. *119* John Selkirk. *121* Fotopress. *123* NZ Rugby Museum. *125* Photosport. *127* M Photosport, Me Auckland Rugby Football Union. *129* Photosport. *131* Photosport. *133* M NZ Rugby Museum, Me NZ Rugby Museum. *135* Bob Howitt Collection. *137* M News Media (Auckland), I Neville Lodge Estate. *138* NZ Rugby Museum. *139* NZ Rugby Museum. *140* A NZ Rugby Museum, B NZ Rugby Museum. *140–1* NZ Rugby Museum. *141* A NZ Rugby Museum, B Pro Sport Photos.

143